TEXAS DRIVER'S PRACTICE HANDBOOK

PUT YOUR BEST FOOT FORWARD TO PASS YOUR TEST

BEN TRIVET

© **Copyright 2020 - All rights reserved.**

The content contained within this book may not be reproduced, duplicated, or transmitted without direct written permission from the author or the publisher.

Under no circumstances will any blame or legal responsibility be held against the publisher, or author, for any damages, reparation, or monetary loss due to the information contained within this book either directly or indirectly.

Legal Notice

This book is copyright protected. This book is only for personal use. You cannot amend, distribute, sell, use, quote, or paraphrase any part of, or the content within, this book, without the consent of the author or publisher.

Disclaimer Notice

Please note the information contained within this document is for educational and entertainment purposes only. All effort has been executed to present accurate, up-to-date, and reliable, complete information. No warranties of any kind are declared or implied. Readers acknowledge that the author is not engaging in the rendering of legal, financial, medical, or professional advice. The content within this book has been derived from various sources. Please consult a licensed professional before attempting any techniques outlined in this book.

By reading this document, the reader agrees that under no circumstances is the author responsible for any losses, direct or indirect, which are incurred as a result of the use of the information contained within this document, including, but not limited to, errors, omissions, or inaccuracies.

CONTENTS

Introduction   v

1. Setting Your Expectations   1
2. The Best Ways to Learn   13
3. Important Laws to Know   26
4. Practice Questions   34
5. Foundational Information You Need to Know   85
6. Test-Taking Strategies   93
7. Answers to Practice Questions   105
8. Driving Test Strategies   126
9. Additional Resources   138

Conclusion   153
References   155

INTRODUCTION

Are you getting ready to take the Texas Driving Exam? If you are, then you absolutely need this book to help you get ready. That's because the exam is going to ask you a lot of detailed questions that are designed to test your knowledge and background on the laws, regulations, and responsibilities for drivers in Texas.

When it comes to preparing for the exam, you want to make sure you're doing everything you can to understand what's expected of you and what's about to come. After all, you don't want to be the only one of your friends not to pass the driving test, right? Well then, you'll need to do a little bit of studying, so you don't just 'wing it' when you get there on test day.

Each question on the exam is meant to determine whether or not you will be a safe and responsible driver on the road. Think of all the people that you care about who are on the road every single day. You want the people driving around them to know how to do it properly, right? Because that's how your friends and family and loved ones stay safe every day.

Well, that's why the State of Texas is going to make you take a driving exam, to test how safe you will be on the road. And that means how secure you will be for yourself as well as for all the other drivers, passengers, pedestrians, and more that will be on or near the road at any given time. If you're not fully prepared for the situations that could arise, you could be a danger to yourself or others.

In this book, we're going to talk about all of the different things you need to know in order to be successful on your driving test. That means we're going to look at the laws and regulations that pertain to not just driving in general but passing your exam. After all, since passing your driver's education course, are you really driving the way you should be?

Chances are that if you're like most people, you stopped driving precisely by the book as soon as you got the paper in your hand that said you had completed driver's training. Even during your practice driving, you may not follow all of the rules exactly the way they're written. In fact, a lot of drivers don't. But when you take the exam, you need to know what the rulebook says.

When you take your exam, you need to remember all of the rules. That means all the things that you were supposed to learn in driver's training and that you should be doing now. Things like how far from a corner you should put on your blinker or how fast you should be driving on a rural road.

All of these things will influence your results. If you don't remember them, you need to do even more studying to make sure that you do when you sit down for the exam. We're going to help with that by going over some of the most essential rules, laws, and regulations and also some of the most commonly asked questions from the exam.

What You'll Find

Let's take a minute to go over what you're going to find in the rest of this book, chapter by chapter. That way, if you're looking for a little extra help with a specific part of your preparations, you can jump right to it and come back to the rest later.

Just make sure you do come back to the rest because you're going to need all of this information to do your best and get the score you need to pass. There are a total of nine different chapters in this book, so make sure you take the time you need before test day to fully explore each one for as long as it takes to feel confident that you understand the material.

In the first chapter, we will talk about setting your expectations for test day. We'll talk about getting prepared and what you should know about the experience as a whole when you walk through the door. This chapter is designed to get you prepared for the experience of testing.

The second chapter will look at some of the best ways that you can learn and study for your exam. We're going to help you with that part, but some people learn in entirely different ways, which means you may want to look at some alternative methods or additional options before you get too close to test day.

Chapter three will look at some of the most important laws and regulations that you need to know when it comes to driving. We'll talk about some of the ones you definitely know as well as some that you may not be as familiar with. We'll go over what these laws mean and how they could affect you on test day.

In chapter four, we're going to get into the real nuts and bolts of this book. This is where we're going to put all the questions that you should be studying in order to pass your written exam. In fact, we're going to include 400 questions that could be on your Texas Driving Exam to make sure that you're well prepared when you sit down with your test.

In chapter five, we'll look at some of the fundamentals of driving and the driving exam that are going to help you with finding the right answer. These fundamentals are some of the things that you already know but that you might find your mind blanking on when it comes time to write them down. We'll help you to make sure that you remember.

Next, in chapter six, we'll look at some of the strategies that you need to know to ace the test. This is the foundational knowledge that is going to help you with taking the exam but doesn't necessarily pertain to the questions themselves. Instead, we're going to look at test-taking strategies and tips that will allow you to do well and remain calm when you start your test.

In chapter seven, we'll give you all the answers to the questions from chapter four. That way, you can test yourself and see just how much you actually know. You'll also be able to practice with these questions again and again until you feel confident that you'll get them right on test day.

Chapter eight is going to get you on the road as we go over some of the strategies that you need to think about when it comes to the driving portion of your test. We're going to take a little bit of time to go over what it's going to take to pass this section, what you may be asked to do, and how you can make sure that your driving score is good enough to pass.

And finally, chapter nine will look at some of the additional resources you may want to explore in order to really get yourself ready and make sure that you're going to do your best on test day. These resources include additional books, websites, and more that will give you more information and advice to study.

Getting Started

Do you feel like you're ready to get started now? Well, hopefully, you are because now it's time to venture into the main part of the content of our book and get you started on the right track when it comes to your driving test.

Remember, you already know all this information because you learned it in your driver's education programs. You just need a refresher course to make sure that you're ready to walk into that building and sit down with your exam.

If you want to walk out of that driver's test with a certificate to get your driver's license, then you can't just walk in and expect to do fine without preparing. Did you take your SAT or ACT in high school without preparing? Did you take your final exams or your entrance exam for college without preparing? Absolutely not. You knew that those were necessary tests that were going to have a significant impact on your life, and so you decided to take the initiative and prepare.

Your driving test is another vital exam in your life. So make sure you're not leaving it up to chance. Take a little bit of time to read through this book, answer the questions a few times, and check out some of the other resources that we've laid out for you. It's definitely going to get you better prepared and help you get the outcome you want for test day.

So, let's dive into what you need to know and get started with the fundamentals that will help you prepare yourself for what's about to come.

1

SETTING YOUR EXPECTATIONS

When it comes to preparing for your driver's test, you want to make sure you're fully equipped for the experience. Remember, this is an essential exam for you because being able to drive symbolizes a sort of rite of passage. Sure, you can be 16 and not have a driver's license, but do you really want to be? Or if you're older and getting your license for the first time, do you want to continue not being able to drive even longer?

The first thing to do is to make sure you know what to expect. When you're walking into that room on test day, you need to be fully prepared because it is an important test, and you want to do well. You are able to retake the test if you don't make it the first time, but who wants to sit for a long examination a second time? Or be without that license you've been waiting for? That's why it's important to know what you're doing the first time around.

So, let's start by looking at the different types of licenses that are offered in Texas. You're going to be applying for your first license, which is the Learner License, but we're going to do a quick overview of each of the different license types so you know what's coming next or what you may be able to apply for further down the line.

Learner License

The first license you'll likely be able to get is a Learner License. We will actually not be focusing on this license throughout the rest of this book because this license still requires you to have an adult in the vehicle. It's not the type of license that allows you to drive alone, even with some restrictions, but we'll get to that in a moment.

Now, the Learner License requires you to be between 15 years and 17 years of age. You also need to have completed at least six hours of your driver's education course. This is because there are two different methods that you can use to get your license and complete driver's education.

The first is the concurrent method. In this process, you would get your Learner License after finishing the first six hours of your driver's education course. For the block method, you would complete the entire 32 hours of the driver's education course and then apply for your Learner License. The rest of the requirements for either program are the same; however, some prefer the option to take care of both at the same time.

You are required to have earned your high school diploma or an equivalent, be enrolled in high school with at least 90% attendance, be enrolled in a program to complete a diploma equivalency test, or be able to prove attendance the previous year for students enrolling in a program during the summer.

You must have a licensed driver who is over the age of 21 in the front seat at all times while driving and must maintain the Learner License for at least six months without suspension prior to applying for the Provisional License. If the license is suspended for any time, the minimum length of time to have the license will be increased so that you have the license and are able to drive for a period of six months.

If you do not apply for the Provisional License, the Learner License will expire on your 18th birthday.

In order to apply for this license, you must have proof of US citizenship or lawful presence, Texas residency, identity, Social Security number, insurance, completion of driver's education program, verification of enrollment and attendance from your high school, and vehicle registration. They must also fill out the application and make an appointment for the remainder of the process.

Provisional License

If you are applying for the Provisional License, you are required to have had your Learner License for at least six months. You must also be between 16 and 17 years of age. Also, you will need to have completed all of the behind-the-wheel portions of the driver's education program, including 7 hours of watching the instructor, 7 hours of observation driving and demonstration, and 30 hours of behind-the-wheel driving practice.

You will need to complete the Impact Texas Teen Driver Program within 90 days of the skills test and successfully pass the driving test. On top of this, your license will still have limitations. These include the fact that you will not be able to drive more than one person who is under the age of 21 and not a family member and you must not drive between midnight and 5 am except in specific circumstances.

This license expires on your 18th birthday if you do not get a Full License before that time.

In order to apply for this license, you must fill out the application and bring a parent or guardian with you. You also must have proof of US citizenship or lawful presence, Texas residency, identity, Social Security number, insurance, completion of driver's education program, verification of enrollment and attendance from your high school, completion of the Impact Texas Driver Program, and vehicle registration.

You will also need to pass a vision test and make an appointment for the rest of the process.

Full License

When it comes to applying for your Full License, you will need to make sure that you have already completed all of the steps above, going through the Learner License and the Provisional License, or that you are over the age of 18. If you fit these qualifications, you will be able to apply for your Full License.

You will need proof of US citizenship or lawful presence, Texas residency, identity, Social Security number, and vehicle registration and insurance, as well as proof of completion of the Impact Texas Driver Program and either a standard driver education course or the six-hour adult driver education course.

In order to receive this license, you must fill out the application, provide all documentation, be fingerprinted, and complete a vision, knowledge, and skills test. This includes a document test as well as a driving test.

Motorcycle/CDL

Texas also offers licenses for motorcycles and CDL, which each have separate requirements in order to apply. Motorcycle licenses are available to anyone who is at least 15 years of age and has completed a driver education course and/or has a Learner License. On the other hand, a CDL can only be awarded if you already have a Texas Full License.

Other requirements apply for both of these types of licenses, and applicants may be required to complete additional testing.

Where to Get Certified

One thing to know about Texas' requirements for driving is that you don't have to do everything at the DMV or any specific DL office. Instead, you can take the driving test and the knowledge test with a third-party provider and bring all of the information to pass this to the DL office in order to get a Provisional or Full License.

This can be a benefit for you because it means you have a little more freedom over where you go and how you're going to get through the entire process. If you're interested in going to the DL office, you can absolutely do so. You need to set up an appointment in order to be able to take the knowledge test as well as the driving test.

If you need to take the test in other languages, you will need to let them know this at the time you schedule as well.

For those who opt to complete all of the testing at a third-party location, you will need to choose which location you want to work with. Keep in mind that you can't just go wherever you want and expect that it's going to work for your certification. You need to make sure that you choose a location that is authorized through the Texas DL office.

If you complete your testing at a location that is not authorized, you will need to retake the tests, and your earlier results will not count. That means it's definitely worth it for you to find an authorized location the first time. Otherwise, you're going to be out a whole lot of time and money trying to get ready for that DL office appointment.

The Texas DL office provides a Third-Party Skills Testing Program, which allows all certified driver education schools to offer the driving test. You will only be able to get a Class C, non-commercial driver's license with this driving test, and it's meant to ensure that you have all of the skills necessary to be a safe motor vehicle operator. Not only that, but it means you won't have to wait around for the DL office.

Now, there are some requirements that you need to keep in mind if you are going through a driver education school to complete your road test. These vary depending on the age of the applicant, so let's take a look.

16 and Older — Youth that are 16–18 years old will need to have a DE-964, which proves that they have completed the Minors Driver Education Course. They will also need to prove that they have had a Learner License for at least six months, and then they will need to complete the Impact Texas Teen Drivers video within 90 days of the date they will take their driving test.

18–24 — Those who are at least 18 but not yet 24 years of age will be required to have a DE-964 or an ADE-1317, which shows that they have completed a driver education course. They will also need to have a valid license that is still a restricted license and complete the Impact Texas Young Drivers video. This must be completed within 90 days of the date that they will take the driving test.

25+ — Those who are over 25 years of age will need to have a valid license that is still a restricted license and will need to complete the Impact Texas Young Drivers video. This must be completed within 90 days of the date that they will take the road test. Drivers over the age of 25 are not required to have taken any driver education courses. While it is recommended, these adults are able to take a driving test to obtain their license with only the Impact Texas Young Drivers video and a restricted license.

Several different driver education schools are authorized to provide this service and allow you to take the driving test. Each individual school is allowed to set the fee for their driving test, and this is not in any way regulated by the Texas Department of Public Safety (DPS). This means you may want to call around in order to find the lowest fees for a program that is authorized by the department.

If you visit the Texas Department of Public Safety website, you can select your county and find an authorized third-party skills testing school in your area. You can also do your own research in your area to see which schools offer driving tests, but make sure that you ask to see proof of their authorization with the

Texas Department of Public Safety. The department will not give you credit for taking a test with an unauthorized facility.

What You Need to Know

Keep in mind that not everyone passes their driving test or their knowledge test on the first try. You may be able to do so and join the many people who are successful in this process, but you may not. That doesn't mean that you should give up or that you should expect to fail when you walk through the door. Rather, it means that you need to prepare yourself fully for what you're going to do.

Going through this book as well as other resources to help you prepare will be the best thing that you can do. Don't try to cram everything at the last minute or assume that you know everything that you need to know so there's no reason to study. Anyone who is looking to take these exams should be studying for them, no matter how long they may have already been driving.

The truth is, these tests are designed to be difficult. But they're not intended to be impossible or to trick you. Rather, the goal is to make sure that you have the knowledge of what you're supposed to be doing and that you can apply it in a real-life situation. You can absolutely do well and get a passing score, but you don't have to be a perfectionist about it either. Passing does not necessarily mean a perfect score.

While you're in the process of setting your expectations, keep in mind that there are some places where the driving test may be a little better than others. Every authorized program has set requirements of things that you have to do and ways that they have to score, but some will provide a little more leeway than others, which means you may want to talk with other people you know who have already taken the test to see what they have to say.

These people might be able to tell you which driving instructors were rigorous and which ones were a little bit more lenient about things. Some instructors might not allow you to pass for any minor discrepancy. Others might give you a little grace about things like the first time you speed (giving you a warning instead of marking you down) or if you turn into the wrong lane on a multilane street (again giving a warning).

If you're taking a driving test, you're definitely going to want to know these things and be able to choose someone who won't fail you immediately for something that you could change with a warning. But that doesn't mean you're going to find someone who will let you get away with driving however you want. You will need to make a few changes if you've been driving for a long time.

That's because when we've been driving for a while a lot of us pick up little habits that might not be entirely correct. What you learned in driver education and what you read throughout this book are the way that you should be answering questions and taking your driving test. But it may not be the way that you've grown accustomed to driving. Be sure that you're following the actual rules when you get behind the wheel or when you answer any questions about the rules.

When you sit down for your knowledge test, you will also need to set your expectations. There is no gray area with this process because questions are either right or wrong. That means you need to have a strong understanding of the rules and regulations related to driving, which is going to be the primary focus of the rest of this book. From there, make sure that you answer all of the questions based on the facts and the laws rather than on what you or someone else may do when driving.

Getting It Right

If you're ready to start preparing for your driving test and your knowledge test, you're in the right place. The next chapter is going to give you some information about different ways you may be able to learn and different options when it comes to studying for all aspects of your testing process. From there, you'll be able to get started actually learning the material and preparing yourself for what's to come.

Don't get too hard on yourself about preparing and passing on the first try. Of course, that's what you want, but if you put too much pressure on yourself, it's only going to make it harder for you to achieve that goal. Instead, just focus on learning the material and practicing as much as you can. That way, you can feel a little more relaxed and a little more comfortable when your test day comes.

Putting a lot of pressure on yourself is definitely not going to help you set expectations in a positive way. Instead, it's going to make you feel anxious, overwhelmed, and potentially even downright terrified. That's not going to help you remember the information that you need to know, and it's not going to help you pass the test. And that will make you feel even worse, putting even more pressure on you for the next time.

Staying relaxed while still taking the time and effort to study and prepare thoroughly for the exams is going to be extremely important. You'll be able to walk in on test day without too much of that overwhelming nervousness, but also without feeling too cocky either. The key is to be confident, but not overly confident, because that could lead you to make foolish mistakes thinking that you already know everything you need to know.

Finding that balance is what the rest of this book is all about. We're going to help you take the edge off your anxiety and confusion about the driving and knowledge tests. But we're going to help you stay humble in the process. So, you can walk in on test day ready and relaxed. All you have to do is keep reading and find out more about the different methods that you can use to learn and study the material that we're going to present in the later chapters.

2

THE BEST WAYS TO LEARN

Are you ready to start studying for your driving test and your knowledge test? We're primarily going to focus on the knowledge test within this book, but we will have some information for you about the driving test as well. That includes the best way to learn for the driving test.

Practice

This probably comes as no surprise, but if you want to do well on the driving test portion of your exam, you're going to need to drive. But you don't just want to get behind the wheel and drive in general. You're going to need to work on some very targeted practice based on the things you'll be tested on and the way that you're going to be tested.

Remember, most people don't drive the way that the law and the driving test are going to say that you should. That means you need to know all of the rules, regulations, and laws that apply to your driving before you get behind the wheel for anything that relates to practicing for your driving test.

Also, pay attention to the specific skills that you're going to be required to do. That means you're probably not going to just drive back and forth to the grocery store or school (with a licensed driver, of course). Rather, you're going to have to get out and drive just for practice purposes so you can get used to different things that you may or may not have to do on a regular drive.

You will want to practice things like left and right turns. Practice merging onto and off of the expressway. Practice changing lanes, signaling traffic, and driving on different types of roads such as school zones, rural roads, and city streets. All of these things are likely to be on your test, and you will need to know how to do them correctly, including what speeds you should be going and how you need to signal each move.

Create a Study Schedule

You want to start creating a study schedule long before you're actually ready to take the test. You may even want to begin a study schedule when you're first getting started with the driver education course you're taking. That way, you can make sure you're prepared to take the knowledge test as soon as you can.

Your study schedule should be realistic, which means you should think about just how much you will actually be able to study each day or each week and lay it out in a way that you can easily follow. Keep in mind that you will have busy days where there are a lot of other things that you need to do. If you're not careful about the way you write your schedule, it could end up being too ambitious, and you'll find yourself falling behind, which could make you feel overwhelmed.

Another essential factor for your study schedule is to put it in writing. Don't just say you're going to study 20 questions each day. Write it on a calendar. Don't say you're going to practice driving for an hour; write it down. When you can look at your calendar every day and see what you're supposed to be doing, it will make you actually do it. Not to mention it gives you something to mark off every day, which helps you feel like you've accomplished something significant.

The best way to create a study schedule is to look at how much or what you want to study and how long you have to do it. Then, divide it out evenly over the number of days you have. This is going to make sure you don't have to do too much in any single day. When you look at the numbers broken down, it's going to look a whole lot easier and a whole lot less daunting as well.

Use Flashcards

Flashcards are great for question and answer study because you can write whatever questions you want on the first side and the answers on the back. This makes it easier for you to study alone or with a partner. Just make sure that you're writing out the questions in a way that's similar to how they will appear on the test and including accurate answers as well.

One even more interesting thing with flashcards is the options. You can actually write out flashcards on notecards or pieces of paper, or you can get an app or program on your computer that will let you record everything. Either option is going to be great, but it's going to be up to you which way you prefer to go.

If you want to write out your own flashcards, you will have a bit more work involved, but some people find that the process of writing the cards actually makes them remember better. You will also have something you can take with you wherever you go, but they take up more space, the more questions you want to practice. That means you may only want to take that day's questions with you when you go somewhere.

On the other hand, putting your flashcards into an app or program makes it faster and easier for most. Some people do well remembering the things that they type, or if your handwriting isn't the greatest, this may help you study, whether alone or with a partner. Not to mention you can take all of your flashcards with you, no matter where you go and no matter how many cards you have. That makes it easier for you to study while you're on the go. And there's no danger of losing your cards.

Take Practice Tests

It is absolutely essential to take practice tests when you're studying. This is different from the flashcards that you're using because instead of going back and forth to look at the question and then the answer, you'll sit down and answer a set number of questions like if you were taking the official test. Then you'll be able to see your answers at the end.

A practice test is going to help you gauge just how you're doing with your practice, and it's going to help you figure out where you need to spend a little more time. The first practice test that you take should be done before you even start studying. This is where you're going to get a good baseline and see just how much you already know. If you do well on certain types of questions and not so well on others, you know where to spend more of your time.

Don't get discouraged if you don't do well at all on the first practice exam that you take. Instead, brush it off and know that you still have a lot of time to study. On the other hand, don't get too cocky if you do really well on the first practice test you take. There are a lot of potential questions that you could get on the exam, and just because you did well on this set of random questions doesn't mean you're going to do as well on all types of questions.

Once you've taken that first practice test, you'll want to scatter other ones throughout your practice. This helps you gauge your progress and also gives you a little more feel for what it's going to be like on test day. That's important because it's going to feel entirely different than flipping through flashcards on the bus. You want to feel prepared for the testing process as well as the questions.

Make sure you also take a practice test right before test day. This will let you know any last-minute items you need to take a look at and will also give you one last chance to get comfortable with the format and style of the exam before you walk in.

Get a Study Partner

Don't try to study entirely by yourself. Instead, take the time to find someone else that you can study with. You probably have an entire class of fellow students who are also preparing to take the test. So, why not enlist one of them to help you? Or how about finding a friend or a family member who is willing to work with you so you can pass your test? Chances are, there's at least one person in your life ready and willing to help.

Your study partner needs to be someone who is going to hold you accountable. That means they need to know what your study schedule is and make sure that you stick to it. They can't be the kind of friend who will tell you it's okay to blow off your studying. And they definitely can't be the kind to tell you that it's not essential to study. You need someone who will push you even when you really don't want to do it.

If they also have to take the exam, this becomes easier because they have a vested interest in you studying as well. They want to pass their own test, and if you're helping them, it's going to be a lot easier for them to do that. You just need to make sure you know which areas each of you needs to study so you can help with those areas. Chances are you're not going to have the same areas that you struggle with, and that means you can help each other remember the information.

You may find that having more than one study partner is the way to go. If you have a few different partners to work with, you'll reap the benefits of different learning styles as well as different skillsets. You'll also be able to set up study groups where everyone is working at the same time. This can reduce the chances of skipping a session because your study partner can't make it at the last minute.

If you have a group and one person doesn't show up, then the rest of you still feel motivated to continue. If there are only two of you and one doesn't show up, you may not be as motivated to do what you know you're supposed to be doing.

Don't Get Overwhelmed.

One of the biggest problems that a lot of people face is getting overwhelmed. It's easy to do, especially when you're talking about something as crucial as getting your license. If you try to cram too much studying into any one day or you put too much pressure on yourself to memorize specific information that you're struggling with too quickly, it could cause overwhelm.

Instead, you want to give yourself a little bit of grace and a whole lot of compassion. Take plenty of breaks while you're working, so you don't feel like you're just pushing, pushing, pushing. And make sure on those breaks you're actually walking away, rather than just leaning back in your chair or setting the papers down for a few minutes.

When you take a little break, it's definitely going to help you feel better about yourself and about your studying. It also gives all of that information at least a little bit of time to sink into your mind, so you're ready to start working on the next bit of information. If you just keep trying to go, go, go, you could find yourself forgetting more than you remember.

Getting overwhelmed is also going to get you frustrated, and you could find yourself making silly mistakes or having trouble remembering things you were confident about before. By taking a little bit of time to relax every so often, you can help yourself avoid this type of burnout and still get all of the studying in that you need for the day.

Teach Someone Else

Teaching someone else may seem strange when you don't quite have a handle on things yourself, but all you need to do is be a little further ahead than the person you're going to teach. That means you may want to help out students who are just getting started with their studying or those who are still in driver education courses because you already know a little bit more than what they know.

When you teach someone, you're forced to remember the information in a way that is a little different, and you may even be surprised by how much you remember. All you need to do is find a student that you can work with. From there, you'll be able to continue studying and learning more information because you want to teach your student rather than just because you're trying to teach yourself. And that can actually help you learn better.

Use Repetition

Sometimes you just need to go over something again and again in order to remember it. Maybe you want to keep going through those flashcards or keep reading the chapter in your book. Or perhaps you just want to write out the questions and answers in list format so you can read through them again and again.

For some people, this is the best way to learn and if that's you, then definitely make sure you're using your skills. Repetition does mean you're going to be going over the same information a lot. And that can be a little boring for some people so look for ways that you can reduce your boredom.

You may not want to read the same chapter one time after another after another. Maybe you want to read a few chapters, then take a little time off and then go back to it. Perhaps you want to go through those 20 flashcards and then do something fun before you go through them again. It's entirely up to you to decide what you want to do and just how you're going to do it.

Look It Up

If you're trying to go through questions and answers or take a practice test and you don't know the answer, struggling through is probably not the way to go. All that's going to do is leave you frustrated, anxious, upset, or any number of other negative emotions. Instead, just admit that you don't know and look up the answer.

If you keep struggling, you're going to end up even worse off than you were previously. But if you take a few minutes to try (and actually try) but still can't get it, then look it up, read through the question and answer a couple of times to get it better in your mind, and then move on to the next one.

You're going to feel more relaxed with this process even though you had to admit that you couldn't do it and had to look up the answer than you would if you kept struggling for 20 minutes or longer and eventually remembered. The key is to make studying as easy as possible, and that's not going to happen if you're stressed.

Use Textbooks/eBooks

There are plenty of different books out there that will help you learn more about the driving test, both the knowledge portion and the actual driving portion. The key is to find books that are going to give you the information that you need, like this one.

We're going to go over tips and techniques like the ones in this chapter as well as practice questions, laws, and more. You want to look for other books that are going to help you focus on the information that you need to know. But make sure they're books that you're actually going to read and work through. The best book in the world won't help you if you don't actually read it.

Try Multiple Methods

Next, make sure you're trying more than one method to learn the material. While it's always a good idea to opt for a learning method that works for you, it's also vital that you try a couple of different options. That's because when you learn in more than one way, you're actually activating different parts of your brain, which means you'll have a better chance of remembering the material.

That might mean spending a little time reading books to learn information (like this one) and then using flashcards or teaching someone else and then taking practice tests. The more different options you use, the better it's going to be for you and your memory overall, so you're definitely going to have the benefits that you're looking for.

You'll be able to practice the same information in all of those different ways as well, which is crucial when you're taking your driving exam. You want to be sure that you have all the right knowledge and a strong foundation for everything you need to learn.

Get Focused

The final tip we have for you is to just sit down and focus. If you're trying to pay attention to your studies, but you're also getting distracted by other things around you, it's definitely not going to help you get where you need to be. You'll find yourself pulled away from your studies too frequently, and, the next time you take a practice test, you just might realize that you haven't gotten as far as you thought.

Staying focused means turning off the radio, the TV, the movies, your phone, or anything else that you might get distracted by. It also means paying attention only to studying for your driving test rather than studying for this test plus your science test and maybe that math homework while you're at it.

You need to be completely focused on only one thing at a time in order to really remember the information. Otherwise, you might find yourself thinking about math while you're supposed to be taking your driving knowledge test. That's definitely not going to help you pass, and it is going to make you feel more stressed out and confused about the answers.

Many people feel like they can multitask just fine and that they learn better that way. The truth is your brain isn't capable of focusing on tasks that way. It can't go from one thing to another to another, and it can't think about multiple things at once. So, if you're trying to do two tasks at the same time, you're going to find yourself forgetting or getting distracted. And if you're jumping from one to the next, you're spending extra time getting your brain to focus each time.

Take the time to focus on only one thing, and then the next thing and then the next, as you finish each task. It's going to help you perform better in practice as well as in your actual test, and that's what the whole point is, right?

3

IMPORTANT LAWS TO KNOW

When it comes time to take the driving test and the knowledge test, there are a number of different laws that you need to know. These are laws that may be on your test or that you may need to refer to while you're driving. That's why we're going to go through some of them so you can be prepared if you're asked.

Running a red light is against the law in Texas, and yet it is one of the most commonly broken laws in the state. This violation can cost $75 to $200 depending on the situation and whether you are caught by a camera or a police officer. Unfortunately, this is the type of infraction that you are definitely likely to get pulled over for because it's easy for officers to write up a ticket, and it can help them get the number of tickets they're supposed to have for a month.

The best thing you can do is keep a close eye on the lights as you approach them. In most cases, you'll be able to see the light turn yellow, and you should be able to stop before the light turns red. If you are too close to the light, you should still take a close look at whether you can make it through the light before it turns to red. If you can, you may be able to go (though generally this is not advised). If you can't, you should do what you can to stop safely before the light.

Using your phone while driving is illegal in many parts of Texas, and it's important to know what the specific law is regarding cell phone use in the areas that you drive. It is your responsibility to know whether you are allowed to use your phone or not and to what extent. In general, there are three different types of ordinances that pertain to phone use. These include an outright ban on all wireless communication devices while driving, a ban on texting while driving, or a ban on texting or manual use of the phone while driving.

If you are caught engaging in any of these actions, you could see a fine from $200 up to $500 depending on where you are and which law you break. The best thing you can do is avoid using your phone at all while driving in Texas, but if you absolutely need to, make sure you know what the law is in the specific area of the state that you're driving in.

Next, driving without a seatbelt is a very common infraction in Texas, which may be because Texas has some of the strictest laws regarding this. All individuals who are in the vehicle must be wearing a seatbelt at all times. This includes the driver, front-seat passenger(s), and rear-seat passengers. Anyone who is not wearing a seatbelt could receive a fine of up to $200.

It's essential to always wear your seatbelt when you're in the vehicle and to make sure that everyone around you does as well. Remember, if you don't wear a seatbelt and you get into an accident, you have a higher chance of being injured or even killed in the accident. These laws are there to protect you, and they help Texas come out as the seventh state in the nation for people wearing seatbelts.

Driving under the influence is another common infraction that you want to avoid getting in the middle of. For drivers under the age of 21, the limit is 0.02. For those who are 21 and over, the limit while driving is 0.08. If you are caught over the limit, you could be fined up to $2,000, be arrested, and be in jail for anywhere from 72 hours to 180 days. Not to mention your license will be revoked for 90 or more days.

All of this means you absolutely want to avoid drinking and driving. While this isn't something that you need to worry about on your driving test, it is something that you may be asked about in the knowledge portion of your exam, so make sure you're paying attention to the specific limits and to the fees and fines you could be responsible for.

Another common infraction is driving without a license. Once again, this isn't one you'll worry about while completing the driving portion of your test because you will have a licensed driver in the vehicle with you for the exam. Make sure that you have your wallet with you that carries your current Provisional or Learner License in it while you're taking your road test.

If you get pulled over and don't have a license, you could have a fee of $200 for a first offense and more for each subsequent offense. Not to mention additional fees and fines. Carrying your license is a simple thing that you can do, and just that one thing will protect you from getting another fee if you're ever pulled over for a different infraction.

Driving without insurance is illegal in Texas, and anyone who does not have insurance will have to pay up to $350 just for that. Plus, you could get a surcharge from the DMV when you go back because you're driving an uninsured vehicle. And that fee could be put on your license for three years. Not to mention each time you're pulled over, you'll have a larger fee, and your vehicle could end up impounded.

Not only are you required to have insurance on your vehicle at all times, but you must have specific limits on your insurance. This includes $25,000 property damage, $30,000 personal injury per person, and $60,000 personal injury per accident. You will have to show proof of insurance before you are able to drive your vehicle for your driving test.

Speeding is one thing that you'll want to be very careful about when it comes to your driving test, and it's something you might be questioned about on your knowledge test. That's because speed limits are generally posted, but you are also required to know the speed limit in specific areas. Fines start at $1 and go up to $200 or more, depending on the severity of the infraction.

If you are speeding excessively or if there are other factors involved, you could even have your license suspended. This means you want to be very careful about how you drive, and you definitely don't want to speed while you're taking your road test. It could result in you being denied your license. Keep in mind, though, that driving safely is the most crucial thing in Texas as their presumed speed limit law means you may be able to drive over the speed limit.

Parking laws vary from one part of Texas to another, so you'll want to look at the regulations in the areas that you're going to be driving in and especially the area where you'll be taking your tests. Parking infractions can actually be quite expensive, and all it takes is a few minutes of leaving your vehicle in the wrong place, and you could be charged.

If you're taking your road test at night or early morning or when the roads are bad, you'll need to be comfortable with using your headlights. You'll also want to know the regulations around this for your knowledge test. The rule is that you should use your headlights if visibility is less than 1,000 feet. Typically, this means 30 minutes after the sunset until 30 minutes before sunrise to make sure you're not jumping it too quickly.

If you don't use your headlights, you could be fined upwards of $200 depending on the area that you're driving in and just how serious the infraction is. If you're only driving without headlights, the fine will be lower than if you are driving without headlights actually causes an accident or an injury to someone else or their property.

Also, keep in mind the laws regarding U-turns. Now, these are allowed in most areas of Texas as long as they can be executed safely. This typically means that you need to be able to see at least 500 feet in front of you and behind you before you make a U-turn. If you can't, you could be pulled over for reckless driving. The same is true if you cause an accident as a result of making a U-turn.

Reckless driving could result in a fine of up to $200, and it could put you behind bars for up to 30 days. That means you need to be very careful about how you're driving and whether you're being safe for yourself and others. It's likely best to avoid making a U-turn while completing your road test unless you are instructed to do so, but you should know the rules about it for your knowledge portion of the test.

You should also know about the different types of licenses, including which one you are going to get. So, let's take a look at what you need to know about the responsibilities and the restrictions that go along with each of the different types of licenses.

A Learner License means you are not allowed to drive unless you have a licensed driver who is over the age of 21 supervising. They must be sitting in the front seat in order to qualify. If you wish to graduate from the Learner License, you must get at least 30 hours of driving time with at least 10 hours of driving time at night.

A Provisional License allows you to drive by yourself, without another licensed adult, but there are still restrictions. You must have no more than one person under 21 in the vehicle at any time unless that person is a family member. You also are not allowed to drive between midnight and 5 am unless you are accompanied by a licensed parent or guardian or if you are going to or from work, school, or a medical emergency.

You are also required to refrain from using an electronic communications device while driving, and you must make sure that all passengers in your vehicle are wearing seatbelts at all times. You are also not allowed to have any amount of alcohol in your system while driving unless over the age of 21.

Once you receive your Full License, there are no new requirements placed on the driver other than those required by law. However, parents may impose rules for children that are living in their household. This could include a parent-teen driving agreement or otherwise.

When it comes to taking your driving test, you need to know everything you can from the Texas Driver Handbook. This book will detail all of the different rules and regulations related to driving in Texas. This includes things like signaling and right-of-way. It has information about different laws that you will need to follow and understand for your knowledge test as well.

While this book is going to go over many of the things you need to know, the Driver Handbook is going to be important as well, and you will want to review the handbook at least a few times when you are studying for the exam. It will help you to get a better handle on everything that's going to apply to both your test and after.

In general, you will be judged on your ability to control your vehicle and observe what is happening around you as well as acting appropriately according to those observations. Not only that, but you'll need to stay in your lane and use your signals properly. This is not all, however. You'll also want to be able to perform different maneuvers.

Parallel parking, quick stops, stopping at both lights and stop signs, following right-of-way laws, straight-line backing, and safely approaching intersections as well as turning correctly. Practice each of these things according to the rules in the Driver Handbook as well as the information in this book. You'll be able to brush up on each of the different techniques according to the regulations for Texas.

4

PRACTICE QUESTIONS

In this chapter we are going to go over some of the many questions that you might have on your knowledge test to get your license. You'll have 400 total questions here and in chapter seven you'll be able to see what the answers are.

Use these questions to help you prepare for what you might see on your exam.

1. If you are driving faster than the other traffic on a freeway, you should use _____.

2. When a vehicle's tires lose contact with the roadway and rise up on top of the water, the condition is called _____.

3. When you approach a railroad crossing that a train is approaching, you must stop your vehicle _____ from the nearest rail.

4. At night, you should dim your headlights to low beam whenever you are _____.

5. If your vehicle is equipped with airbags, you should use _____ to turn the steering wheel in most driving situations.

6. When approaching an intersection where there are no signs or traffic lights, you must _____.

7. In Texas, you must use your headlights from one half hour after sunset until _____.

8. In Texas, you must parallel park your vehicle within _____ of the curb or edge of the roadway.

9. If a broken yellow line is on your side of the centerline _____.

10. If an emergency vehicle is approaching you with its siren, bell, or flashing red lights on, you must _____.

11. When you approach a flashing yellow light at an intersection, you should _____.

12. Under Texas law, if you intend to turn, you must signal continuously for at least _____ before you turn.

13. _____ on your side of the road indicates a no-passing zone.

14. If you're driving at night in fog or heavy rain, use _____.

15. Under Texas law, you must not park your vehicle _____.

36 | BEN TRIVET

16. In a roundabout, you must drive _____.

17. For drivers who are at least 21 years of age, the legal limit for blood alcohol concentration (BAC) is _____.

18. If a tire blows out, you should _____.

19. To avoid the glare of an oncoming vehicle's headlights, you should shift your eyes _____.

20. In Texas, which occupants of a passenger vehicle must wear safety belts or appropriate child restraints?

21. In which of the following situations should you NOT drive on the left side of the road?

a. When the pavement markings prohibit it

b. When there are two or more traffic lanes in each direction

c. When you're within 100 feet of an intersection

d. When passing a vehicle where the pavement markings allow it

22. When going down a steep hill, you should _____.

23. The stopping distance of an average passenger car traveling at 55 mph is approximately _____.

24. If you approach a school bus from either direction while the bus is displaying alternately flashing red lights, you must _____.

25. In Texas, the speed limit in urban districts is _____ unless otherwise posted.

26. When you're driving on the highway, you can prevent highway hypnosis by _____.

27. At speeds over 30 mph, you should maintain a following distance of at least _____ behind the vehicle ahead of you.

28. _____ may be used in work zones in both day and night to guide drivers into certain traffic lanes.

29. Areas of the road that you cannot see in your mirrors are called _____.

30. Opposing lanes of traffic are separated by _____.

31. In Texas, when is it legal to drive on a paved shoulder to pass another vehicle on the right?

32. To enter a main road from a driveway, an alley, or the roadside, you must _____.

33. When entering or exiting a roundabout, you must _____.

34. Blind pedestrians may carry _____ canes or use the assistance of guide dogs.

35. On a two-way road, a _____ allows you to cross over into the opposing lane temporarily to pass a vehicle if it is safe to do so.

36. On a roadway with three or more lanes going in the same direction, which lanes usually offer the smoothest flow of traffic?

37. In Texas, you may make a left turn at a red light if you are turning _____.

38. Following too closely behind a vehicle is also known as _____.

39. If you see a flag person on the road, it means that _____.

40. Headrests should be adjusted so that the head restraint contacts the back of the head. This prevents _____.

41. If a truck is trying to pass you, you can help the truck driver by _____.

42. To enter a freeway smoothly, enter an acceleration lane and _____ to match the speed of highway traffic.

43. If you are signaled by a flag person at or near a railroad crossing or work zone, you must _____.

44. When you drive through a work zone, you should NOT _____.

45. When entering a main road from a private road, a driveway, or an unpaved road, you must _____.

46. A double solid yellow line in the middle of the road means that passing is _____.

47. On multilane roads, the _____ lane is intended to be used for passing slower vehicles.

48. You must maintain a constant speed when passing and reentering the lane in front of a truck or bus, because trucks and buses require _____.

49. If you're having vehicle trouble at night and need to stop, you should use _____ to avoid an accident.

50. While getting onto a freeway, you reach the end of the on-ramp. At this point, you should be traveling _____.

51. If you see a pedestrian using a guide dog or carrying a white cane, you must _____.

52. When you park and leave your vehicle in the street, you should _____.

53. To enter an expressway or freeway, you must _____ before merging with the traffic.

54. What is the correct hand and arm signal to indicate a left turn?

55. When you come to an intersection, follow the _____ before you proceed.

56. What is the correct hand and arm signal for indicating a right turn?

57. On a multilane freeway, pedestrians should walk _____.

58. Before changing lanes, you should _____.

59. If you are parallel parked on the right side of the street, you should _____ before pulling out into traffic.

60. A sign with black letters on an orange background is _____.

61. Rain, snow, and ice impair your ability to see ahead and can make roads more slippery. To be able to stop safely, you should _____.

62. To avoid last-minute braking or the need to turn

suddenly, you should look at least _____ ahead while driving in the city.

63. A _____ offers you the best possible protection in a car crash and is therefore your best defense against a drunk driver.

64. If a tire suddenly goes flat while you're driving, you should _____.

65. When making a left turn at an intersection or into an alley or driveway, you must yield the right-of-way to _____.

66. When preparing to leave a parallel parking space, you should _____.

67. When two vehicles meet on a steep mountain road where neither can pass, which vehicle has the right-of-way?

68. On a multilane roadway with several lanes in your direction, you must use _____ for passing

69. If you are going to stop or slow down where others might not expect it, you should _____ to warn those behind you.

70. If a broken yellow line is on your side of the centerline _____.

71. A red arrow signal at an intersection indicates that _____.

72. If your engine dies as you're driving on a curve, you should _____.

73. If you are about to pass a bicycle to your immediate

right and an oncoming vehicle is approaching you on your immediate left, what should you do?

74. While you are driving, talking on a cell phone may increase your chances of being in a crash by _____.

75. You can avoid panic stops by _____.

76. A roundabout is a circular intersection in which vehicles travel around a center island in _____ direction.

77. A flashing red signal indicates that you must _____ before going farther.

78. At an intersection, a single solid white line across the road means that you must _____ for a traffic signal or sign.

79. When making a U-turn, you must NOT _____.

80. Tailgating is the practice of _____.

81. The hand and arm bent at 90 degrees and pointing downward indicate the driver's intention to _____.

82. If your rear wheels start to skid, what should you do?

83. When you encounter a truck traveling next to you, keep as far as possible to the side to avoid _____.

84. Rear-end crashes are common on highways because many drivers _____.

85. _____ are usually diamond shaped with black lettering or symbols on a yellow background.

86. At an intersection, a steady yellow arrow signal pointing left means _____.

87. If you are approaching an intersection and see a steady yellow traffic light, you should _____.

88. If you see a yield sign in your lane, you must _____.

89. If it starts to rain on a hot day, use caution because the pavement may be slippery for the first few minutes. This is due to _____.

90. To avoid a head-on collision if there is an oncoming vehicle in your lane, you should _____.

91. To turn around on a narrow, two-way street, you may make _____.

92. A driver who is convicted of DWI will lose his or her driving privileges for at least _____ for a third offense.

93. If you had an accident that resulted in at least _____ in damages to property (including your own), you should fill out a Driver's Crash Report.

94. On a four-lane divided roadway or a one-way road, a solid yellow line usually marks _____.

95. You are driving on a four-lane highway. You see an emergency vehicle pulled over with its lights flashing ahead. What must you do?

96. Unbalanced tires or low tire pressures can cause _____.

97. You may pass a vehicle on the right in the following situations: _____.

98. An adult driver who is convicted of DWI for the first time will lose his or her driving privileges for up to _____.

99. If a driver who is at least 17 years of age but under 21 years of age is convicted of DUI (not DWI) for the third time, he or she may be fined up to _____.

100. If a driver under 21 years of age is convicted of DWI while in possession of an open container of alcohol, he or she will be sentenced to jail for at least _____ for a first offense.

101. An adult driver who is convicted of DWI for the first time will lose his or her driving privileges for at least _____.

102. A driver who is convicted of DWI will be sentenced to jail for at least _____ for a second offense.

103. An adult driver who is convicted of DWI will lose his or her driving privileges for up to _____ for a second offense.

104. What is this sign?

44 | BEN TRIVET

105. What is this sign?

106. What is this sign?

107. What is this sign?

TEXAS DRIVER'S PRACTICE HANDBOOK | 45

108. What is this sign?

109. What is this sign?

110. What is this sign?

46 | BEN TRIVET

111. What is this sign?

112. What is this sign?

113. What is this sign?

114. What is this sign?

115. What is this sign?

116. What is this sign?

48 | BEN TRIVET

117. What is this sign?

118. What is this sign?

119. What is this sign?

120. What is this sign?

121. What is this sign?

50 | BEN TRIVET

122. What is this sign?

123. What is this sign?

124. What is this sign?

125. What do the broken white lines mean?

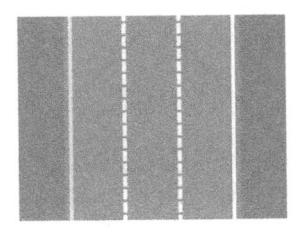

126. What does the solid white line mean?

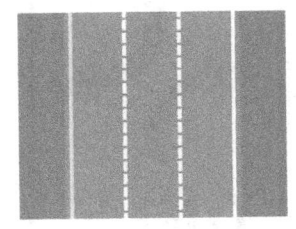

127. What does the solid yellow line mean?

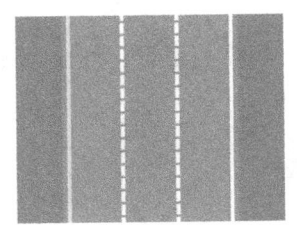

52 | BEN TRIVET

128. What is this sign?

129. What is this sign?

130. What is this sign?

131. What is this sign?

132. What is this sign?

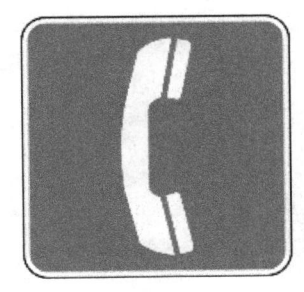

133. What is this sign?

54 | BEN TRIVET

134. What is this sign?

135. What is this sign?

136. What is this sign?

137. What is this sign?

138. What is this sign?

139. What is this sign?

140. What is this sign?

141. What is this sign?

142. What is this sign?

143. What is this sign?

144. What is this sign?

145. What is this sign?

146. What is this sign?

147. What is this sign?

148. When driving on slick roads drivers should _____.

149. To reduce their chances of colliding with an animal, drivers should _____.

150. What is this sign?

151. What are some telltale signs of a drunk driver?

152. What should you do if you see smoke come from under the hood?

153. A driver should be extra alert for motorcyclists, bicycles, and pedestrians. Why?

154. What is the purpose of minimum speed limits?

155. When driving on major highways you should _____.

156. Which shape is a warning sign?

157. Your blind spot is the area of the road _____.

158. Never make a U-turn from _____.

159. You must come to a full stop at a yield sign _____.

160. What does alcohol do to you while driving?

161. A red traffic sign means _____.

162. What is this sign?

163. You should never depend on your mirrors when you prepare to change lanes. Why?
164. The driver of an emergency vehicle that uses lights and a siren can legally _____.
165. A steady yellow light means _____.
166. What should you do as you prepare to turn right at an intersection?
167. When changing lanes, you should _____.
168. For protection, motorcyclists are required to _____.
169. A driver approaching a flashing red traffic signal must _____.
170. Alcohol can impair your driving by _____.
171. Drivers may pass another vehicle if the line dividing two lanes is a _____ line.

172. What is this sign?

173. When driving in bad weather, drivers should _____.

174. Your first response to reduced visibility should be _____.

175. When in a motor vehicle on a highway, it is _____.

176. Are bicyclists required to obey traffic laws and signs?

177. What is this sign?

178. When driving in travel lanes on the roadway, _____.

179. If your turn signals fail, you should use _____ to indicate your intention to turn.

180. Drivers under 21 years of age are considered to be driving under the influence if their blood alcohol concentration (BAC) is _____.

181. At intersections where two or more drivers stop at STOP signs at the same time and they are at right angles, _____.

182. What is this sign?

183. What is this sign?

184. If you stop along the road at night, _____.

185. What is this sign?

186. Destination signs are _____ with ____ letters and symbols.

187. When children are close, what should you do before you back out of a driveway?

188. What does this mean when flashing?

189. When parking on a public road, drivers should _____.

190. What is this sign?

191. If an approaching driver does not dim the headlights, you should _____.

192. What is this sign?

193. _____ is the only effective way to reduce your blood alcohol concentration (BAC).

194. If you are pulled over by law enforcement, you should _____.

195. What is this sign?

196. What is this sign?

197. What is this sign?

198. What is the first thing you should do if your wheels move off the pavement?

199. On average, how long does it take your body to remove the alcohol contained in 5 ounces of wine?

200. Two motorcyclists are allowed to _____.

201. If you are continually being passed on the right, you should _____.

202. When meeting a car with blinding headlights, you should _____.

203. You go with a group of friends to a social event, and you plan to have a few drinks. You should _____.

204. When making a turn, drivers must _____ their speed.

205. Drivers cannot pass a vehicle on the left if _____.

206. When approaching a curve, remember to _____.

207. When you prepare to make a left turn from a one-way road into a two-way road, you must _____.

208. Drivers should use the horn _____.

209. A vehicle that enters a road from a driveway _____.

210. It is important for drivers to know that trucks _____.

211. When a 'Road Closed' sign is displayed, drivers must _____.

212. Drivers may cross solid yellow lines _____.

213. As you approach an intersection, the traffic light changes from green to yellow. You should _____.

214. Anything that requires you to _____ could cause you to crash.

215. Drivers are required to stop _____.

216. When driving in heavy traffic, you should _____.

217. What should you do when you encounter this sign?

218. If the entrance lane is too short to allow acceleration to highway speed, you should _____.

219. A broken yellow line alongside a solid yellow line means _____.

68 | BEN TRIVET

220. What should you do when the red lights on this sign begin to flash?

221. When the road is slippery, you should _____.
222. What does this sign mean?

223. What does this sign mean?

224. What type of pavement marking shows you which lane you must use for a turn?

225. Your brake lights tell other drivers that you _____.

226. Most signs used in street work areas are _____.

227. Green and white signs _____.

228. What does this sign mean?

229. To avoid being in a truck driver's blind spot, you should _____.

230. You are at a red traffic signal. The traffic light turns green, but there are still other vehicles in the intersection. You should _____.

231. If a pedestrian is in a crosswalk in the middle of a block, _____.

232. You must yield the right-of-way to an emergency vehicle by _____.

233. You are going to make a left turn from a dedicated left-turn lane when a yellow arrow appears for your lane. You should _____.

234. You should dim your lights for oncoming vehicles or when you are within 300 feet of a vehicle _____.

235. Following closely behind another vehicle (tailgating) _____.

236. If your cell phone rings while you are driving and you do not have a hands-free device, you should _____.

237. Before driving into an intersection from a stop, you should look _____.

238. When roads are slippery, you should _____.

239. At night, if an oncoming vehicle fails to dim its high beams, look _____.

240. When driving in traffic at night on a dimly lit street, you should _____.

241. If you have a collision, the law requires you to

exchange your driver license information with _____.

242. You want to make a right turn at the corner. A pedestrian with a guide dog is at the corner ready to cross the street in front of you. Before making your turn, you should _____.

243. When backing up in a passenger vehicle _____.

244. If there are two solid yellow lines in the center of the roadway, you _____.

245. When passing another vehicle, it is safe to return to your lane if you _____.

246. What does this sign mean?

WRONG WAY

247. Which way should your front wheels be turned when parked uphill next to a curb?

248. You should always turn on your emergency flashers when _____.

249. If the roadway is wet and your car starts to skid, you should _____.

250. When you enter traffic from a stop (example: pulling away from the curb), you _____.

251. Always look carefully for motorcycles before changing lanes because _____.

252. If you see orange construction signs or cones on a highway or road, you must _____.

253. Do motorcycles have more, less, or the same rights and responsibilities as other motorists?

254. Before getting out of your parked car on the traffic side of the street, you should _____.

255. Generally speaking, you are in a large truck's blind spot if you _____.

256. A flashing red traffic light at an intersection means _____.

257. If you are riding in a vehicle equipped with a lap belt and also a separate shoulder belt, you are _____.

258. If there is no crosswalk and you see a pedestrian crossing your lane, you should _____.

259. Which of the following is true about roadways on bridges and overpasses in cold, wet weather?

a. They tend to freeze before the rest of the road does

b. The speed limit is lower

c. The speed limit is higher

d. They freeze after the rest of the road

260. You want to park uphill on a two-way road and there is no curb. Which way do you turn your front wheels?

261. You reach an intersection with stop signs on all four corners at the same time as the driver on your left. Who has the right-of-way?

262. What does this sign mean?

263. When driving at speeds under 30 mph, keep a minimum following distance of _____.

264. If your wheels drop off the pavement and onto the shoulder of the road, you should _____.

265. When involved in an accident, you should provide _____.

266. A stop sign is shaped like a(n) _____.

267. Don't follow other cars too closely because _____.

268. When driving at speeds faster than 30 mph, keep a minimum following distance of _____.

269. If you miss your exit on an interstate expressway, _____.

270. Defensive drivers should _____.

271. If an officer is directing traffic at a working traffic light, drivers should _____.

272. Always signal when _____.

273. Shared lanes may be used by _____.

274. When making a right turn, you should NOT _____.

275. Railroad crossings should always be considered _____.

276. Night driving can be more difficult than driving during the day because _____.

277. Allow a larger space cushion than usual when stopping _____.

278. At a light rail intersection, always _____.

279. You may park directly across the street from the entrance of a fire station _____.

280. To avoid road rage, it is a good idea to _____.

281. Unless otherwise posted, the speed limit in an alley is _____.

282. While driving on a two-lane road without bicycle lanes, you encounter a bicyclist traveling in the same direction. What is the safest way to pass the bicyclist?

283. When in a travel lane on the roadway _____.

284. You should not park within ____ of an intersection.

285. What does this sign mean?

286. What does this sign mean?

287. When may drivers leave their vehicle unattended with the engine running?

288. If a crossing guard is directing traffic in a school zone, you must _____.

289. Drivers should use their low-beam headlights _____.

290. Before switching on the ignition, you should _____.

291. At night, it is hardest to see _____.

292. What should you do if your accelerator sticks while you are driving?

293. A bicyclist who doesn't obey traffic laws _____.

294. You must not drive your vehicle at a speed greater than _____.

295. A person who drives much slower than the speed limit _____.

296. Which of the following statements about railroad crossings is true?

a. It is against the law to go around lowered gates at a crossing

b. You must stop at a railroad crossing when directed to do so by a flagger

c. Not all railroad crossings are equipped with flashing red signals and gates

d. You should proceed through the intersection if you cannot see the train

297. How often are motor vehicles required to be inspected?

298. Drinking alcohol and driving is _____.

299. What does this sign mean?

300. The most common color of warning signs is _____.

301. Operating a motor vehicle is _____.

302. What helps a person sober up after consuming alcohol?

303. At dusk or on overcast days, you should _____.

304. If you have the right-of-way at an intersection, you should _____.

305. What does this sign mean?

306. A pedestrian starts to cross in front of your vehicle. You should _____.

307. An arrow painted on the pavement means _____.

308. When driving in a construction zone, you should be prepared _____.

309. Which are some side effects that can happen after drinking?

a. Your reflexes and reaction time slow down

b. Your judgement of speed and distance is distorted

c. You are less alert

d. You can drive if you stay slow

310. When a traffic signal light turns green, you should _____.

311. What are some common causes of traffic accidents?

312. Drivers may not park within ____ of a railroad crossing.

313. It is illegal to follow within ____ of a fire truck that is sounding its siren.

314. What must you do when passing?

315. What must you do when starting a passing maneuver?

316. You must stop at an intersection when you see a _____.

317. A "No stopping" sign means that, unless directed to do so by a police officer, you may stop only _____.

318. Driving while being distracted by any activity _____.

319. Fines for moving traffic violations in construction and maintenance zones are _____.

320. You are involved in an accident. You should _____.

321. When approaching a T intersection, drivers _____.

322. You cannot pass safely on a two-way, two-lane street unless _____.

323. Regulatory signs are usually ____ and should always be obeyed.

324. What should you know about emergency vehicles?

325. You are involved in an accident and another person is injured. You should _____.

326. You are driving when it starts to sleet or snow. You should _____.

327. If a pedestrian hybrid beacon signal light is flashing red, it means _____.

328. Refusing to take an alcohol level test when under suspicion of driving while intoxicated or driving under the influence _____.

329. If another car is in danger of hitting you, you should _____.

330. When approaching a flashing yellow light, drivers should _____.

331. A seatbelt should be adjusted so that it _____.

332. The effect that lack of sleep has on your safe driving ability is the same as _____.

333. What is the first thing you should adjust, if needed, when you get into a car to drive?

334. Roads become very slippery _____.

335. When preparing to turn left, drivers should _____.

336. When leaving a parking space, drivers should _____.

337. When turning onto a one-way street, drivers should _____.

338. What does this sign mean?

339. What does a lane control signal with a green arrow above a reversible lane indicate?

340. As a pedestrian, you should _____.

341. A driver entering public traffic from a driveway or private road _____.

342. If your car starts to skid, turn your steering wheel _____.

343. If pedestrian hybrid beacon signal lights are black, it means _____.

344. You are entering a crowded freeway. What should you do to merge into traffic?

345. You can reduce the risk of hydroplaning by _____.

346. Where may drivers deposit their litter while on the roadways?

347. What do large flashing arrow panels indicate?

348. When driving in traffic, it is safest to _____.

349. You should not park within ____ of a traffic control signal.

350. The most effective thing you can do to reduce your risk of being injured or killed in a traffic crash is to _____.

351. When approaching a railroad crossing, you should _____.

352. When should you return to your previous lane while completing a pass?

353. A flashing red traffic signal at an intersection has the same requirements as _____.

354. When entering a highway from an entrance ramp, you should generally _____.

355. You are coming to a railroad crossing where the crossing signals are flashing. You should _____.

356. A regulatory sign containing a red circle with a slash through the middle indicates _____.

357. You must yield for emergency vehicles _____.

358. When is it legal to have an open container of alcohol in a motor vehicle passenger area?

359. When approaching a railroad crossing warning sign _____.

360. A slow-moving vehicle emblem is _____.

361. If you leave your vehicle unattended, you must _____.

362. When passing an emergency vehicle stopped on the side of the road, drivers should _____.

363. Distracted driving is _____.

364. Traffic signals sometimes display arrows to control turns from specific lanes. A solid red arrow _____.

365. Stop lines are solid white lines painted across traffic lanes _____.

366. When driving past a vehicle that has just stopped in a parked position on the side of the road, you should _____.

367. When encountering a warning sign, drivers should _____.

368. When is it acceptable to park in a striped area next to a disabled parking spot?

369. Alcohol-related crashes represent ____ of the total number of persons killed in automotive crashes.

370. If you are driving in another driver's blind spot, you should _____.

371. What does a single dashed white line separating traffic mean?

372. The driver's left arm and hand are extended upward. This hand signal means that the driver plans to _____.

373. Two solid white lines painted across a traffic lane show the boundaries of a crosswalk. As a driver, you should know that _____.

374. What does a lane control signal with a steady yellow X above a reversible lane indicate?

375. Street racing is legal _____.

376. Before turning left, it is important to _____.

377. What does this sign mean?

378. A red and white triangular sign at an intersection means _____.

379. When you approach a railroad crossing without flashing warning signals or crossing gates, you should _____.

380. Unless otherwise posted, the speed limit on a highway is _____.

381. Work zone signs mean _____.

382. When driving on roads that may be slippery _____.

383. A double solid yellow line down the center of a two-lane road indicates _____

384. When driving under icy or snowy conditions, which driving technique will help drivers avoid crashes?

385. You may drive in the HOV lane if _____..

386. What do you do when you see this sign?

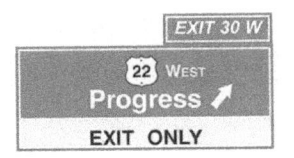

```
EXIT 30 W
22 WEST
Progress ↗
EXIT ONLY
```

387. Unless otherwise posted, the speed limit on county roads adjacent to public beaches is _____.

388. You experience an incident at work that has left

you feeling angry. When you get to your car, you should _____.

389. Signaling your intentions before turning, changing lanes, or driving away from a curb _____.

390. When you see a "merging traffic" sign you should _____.

391. When approaching a roundabout, you should always _____.

392. When passing on a multilane highway you should _____.

393. What are the colors of warning signs indicating upcoming hazards?

394. On a road which has no sidewalks, a pedestrian should walk on the _____.

395. When dealing with an injured person at an accident you should only move them _____.

396. You may pass another vehicle if the line dividing your lane from the lane you wish to enter is a ____ line.

397. When a stop is required at an intersection and no markings appear to indicate a stop line or crosswalk, a driver _____.

398. Highway markings _____.

5

FOUNDATIONAL INFORMATION YOU NEED TO KNOW

In this chapter, we're going to take a look at some of the critical information that you should know about your test before you even walk in the door. This chapter is going to help you understand the way the test experience is going to go and how you can make sure you're getting the best score possible.

Documents You Will Need

First, make sure you have everything that you're going to need in order to get your license. There are a number of documents that you need to provide, and you don't want to be denied the opportunity to take your test after you've studied so much for it just because you forgot one. So, which documents are you going to need and what are they going to do for you?

Texas Learner License — The first thing you will need to have is your current Learner License. This lets the Department of

Public Safety know that you have already gone through the previous portion of your process, including taking the courses (though you will need to have additional proof of that as well).

Your license will serve as a way to confirm your identity and to ensure that you are located properly in the system when they set you up for that exam. Once you receive your Learner License, it should remain in your wallet, purse, or otherwise in your possession at all times.

Test fee — You're going to need to pay a fee in order to take the exam. There are different fees depending on your age. However, if you are looking for a brand new driver's license with no restrictions, you will be required to pay $16 for the license, which will be valid only until your 18th birthday.

There may be other fees or additional costs added to this, so be prepared or call your local office to find out for sure what the cost will be. You can also pre-pay for this online and bring the receipt with you. Make sure you do not wait too long as pre-payment is only valid for 90 days. After that, you will be required to make a second payment, and the first will not be refunded.

Certificate of Completion for ITD — ITD is the Impact Texas Drivers Program, which may be either the teen driver's or young driver's version. These programs are free with the teen driver version intended for those who have completed a teen driver education course. This video is two hours long and shares information about distracted driving and real-life situations that have occurred as a result.

The young driver's version is an hour long and provides similar stories and information about distracted driving and outcomes from it. This video is provided for those who have completed the adult driver education course or who are older than 25 and may or may not have completed any driver education course.

One of these videos and certification to prove completion are required in order to take your driving exam and get your license.

Proof of Driver Education — If you are younger than 25 years of age, you are required to complete either a teen or adult driver education course. In order to get your license, you will need to show proof of completion of this course. This could be in the form of

- Texas Driver Education Certificate DE-964 from a certified driving school,
- Texas Driver Education Certificate DE-964E from a public high school,
- Parent Taught Driver Education Certificate PTDE-964,
- Adult Driver Education Certificate ADE-1317.

Proof of Liability Insurance — You will be taking a road test, which means you need to prove that your vehicle is legally allowed to be on the road. Liability insurance is required, and the individual who will be taking the road test must be listed as a driver on the named driver policy. They cannot be listed as an excluded driver. This means that they are covered under the auto insurance policy.

Rental agreement — If a rental car is being used to take the road test, the individual who will be taking the road test must be listed as an authorized driver. There also must be proof of liability insurance on the rental vehicle specifically or of a family policy of liability insurance that covers the rental vehicle. This will ensure that the car is fully insured and capable of being used with the exam.

The Vehicle

There are specific requirements in place for the vehicle that you will use in the process of your driving test. The vehicle must have current registration, proved by the current registration sticker. It must also have two license plates, with one on the front and one on the rear of the vehicle.

The vehicle must have no unusual mechanical issues and must be able to pass an inspection that will be completed prior to you being able to take the driving test. It also must allow you to complete all of the stages required in the How to Prepare for a Drive Test checklist.

The specific aspects that will be looked at for your vehicle inspection include the following:

- Two license plates. The vehicle must have a license plate on the front and rear bumper in order to be legal to drive in Texas. The only exception to this is a vehicle that has temporary plates or an out-of-state plate, in which case the car must have one plate on the rear of the vehicle. Temporary plates are generally on the rear bumper or in the rear window, while out-of-state plates are on the rear bumper.
- Operational speedometer. The speedometer has to be present, and it needs to function. If it is off by a few miles per hour, this is not cause for alarm; however, if it is very far off or if it doesn't move at all while you are driving, this will not be allowed.
- Properly functioning horn. You are only expected to use the horn to signal to other drivers if there is a reason to notify them of some type of danger; however, your vehicle must have an operational horn in order to pass inspection. You will be required to demonstrate that the horn works before you can go out on the road.
- Operational turn signals. The turn signals for both right and left need to work, and they need to work at both the front and back of the vehicle. You will be asked to demonstrate this before you will be allowed to begin the driving test.
- Unexpired vehicle registration. You will be required to present your registration in order to take the vehicle

out on the road. It must be still valid whether for the State of Texas or for another state if the car has out-of-state plates.

- Unexpired insurance. Your vehicle must be covered under liability insurance, whether it is a vehicle owned by you or your family (or anyone else) or a car that is rented from a rental company. If the vehicle is from a rental company, the individual taking the test must be listed. Otherwise, the person driving the vehicle must not be listed as an excluded driver on the insurance policy.
- One rearview mirror. The rearview mirror can be on the inside or outside of the vehicle, but there must be at least one on the car in order to drive it safely. This mirror will have to be correctly attached and be operational.
- Driver and front passenger doors must open. You and the driving instructor must be able to open your respective doors normally, from outside the vehicle, using the door handle. If the doors do not open properly, this is considered a safety hazard, and you will not be able to complete the test.
- Functioning seatbelts. Texas state law requires that every occupant of the vehicle wear a seatbelt at all times when the car is in operation. This means that your seatbelts must be functioning. They must be

installed correctly, and they must be able to buckle and tighten to the proper fit.
- Brake lights. When you apply the brake, it is essential that anyone outside of your vehicle is able to recognize that you have done so. This will be checked before you are able to leave the parking lot as the driving instructor will check that the rear brake lights on both sides activate when the brake pedal is pushed.
- Headlights and taillights. Just like with the brake pedal, it is essential that your headlights and taillights are fully operational and can be turned on and off properly. The driving instructor will request that you turn on and off these lights and may also ask you to do so while you are completing the driving test to make sure you can do so while driving.
- Windshield wipers. Windshield wipers are required when driving a vehicle in Texas, which means you must have them properly installed and should be able to turn them on and off as needed. You may or may not need to exhibit the use of the windshield washers, but it's a good idea to be comfortable with this as well.

If your vehicle does not pass the inspection or you do not have any of the required documentation, you will be required to come back at a later time. You may also be required to get the vehicle repaired so that it can pass inspection or bring a different car with you that is able to pass the inspection.

Remember, you will also need a licensed driver with you as you are not permitted to drive to the DPS office yourself without a licensed driver. You will still be under the restrictions of the Learner License that you have. Arriving without a licensed driver could also result in being refused the opportunity to take the exam.

Preparing to go to the DPS office is going to be a big step, and it's definitely going to feel like you're more than ready. After all, you've been preparing for this moment for many years now. You spent all that time waiting until you were old enough to drive and then taking driver's education and practicing driving. Now it's time to walk into the office and do what you've been preparing to do: take your written test and your road test. Let's take a look at a few tips that will help you with the other half of getting your driver's license.

6

TEST-TAKING STRATEGIES

When it comes to taking your test, you want to make sure that you are fully prepared. This means making sure that when you walk into the DPS office on the day of your test, you feel comfortable doing so. Make sure that you take a look at each of these test-taking strategies to help you prepare and feel more comfortable when it comes time to take the test.

Be in good shape for the test day. That means you want to get a good night's sleep beforehand, and you also want to eat well before you go in. If you're tired or if you're hungry, you're definitely not going to do as well on your test because that's what you're going to be thinking about. It's only going to make you rush or get overly stressed, and you could struggle to get the questions right.

Know the instructions beforehand. One of the first things that you should do is look for the instructions regarding your test before you get to test day. You want to be comfortable with what's required early on so you can prepare yourself. If you walk in on test day and don't know what you're doing, you're going to feel a lot more nervous, and you may find yourself making mistakes that you wouldn't have otherwise.

Write down notes. You can have a piece of paper with you when you take the exam, but it can't have anything written on it when you sit down. That doesn't mean that you can't write up notes as soon as you do sit down. Anything you find yourself forgetting often, you may want to jot down quickly. Or even just a positive note that lets you know you can do this and that you're going to pass your test.

Read through the instructions. When you get to test day, and you sit down to take the test, don't assume that you know the instructions. Yes, you should have read through them beforehand and should feel comfortable with them but make sure you read through them again. This will help you feel more confident and prepare for the test itself. It will also make sure you don't miss any last-minute changes to the test.

Answer easy questions first. As with any test that you take, you should be answering the easy questions before you try to progress to anything too tricky. Working through the easy questions gives you more confidence because each question you're confident you got right makes you more willing to continue. Not only that, but you're going to move through the test more quickly because you get the easy questions out of the way.

Make note of the hard questions. Make note of which questions you skip over so you can go back to them once you get through the easy questions. Whether you're taking a paper test or an online test, you want to have a blank piece of paper next to you so you can write down the numbers. This makes sure that you won't miss a question when you have to go back through. You don't want to skip answering a question because you forgot it.

Answer every question. You are scored based on how many questions you get right out of the total number of questions asked. You are not scored on how many questions you get right compared to how many you attempt. That means you should answer every single question before you complete your test. There is no penalty for a wrong answer, and you could get the question right even if you have to guess.

Read each question carefully. The purpose of this test is not to trip you up, but if you're reading through the questions and answers too quickly, you might miss something. Instead, read the question carefully, making sure that you read every word. Then choose the answer that best fits the question.

Answer before you read the answers. When you read the question, try to decide on the answer before you even read the options. This will help you feel more confident if the answer you chose is one of the options. You'll be able to pick that answer and then move on to the next question without having to second-guess yourself.

Read every answer. Even if you think you know the answer, you should still read through each of the answers. Sometimes there is more than one answer that is accurate. In that case, you need to choose the best answer to the question. It's also possible that you could read one answer and think it's correct, then realize that another answer is more accurate according to what's asked.

Answer the question. Don't just assume you know what the author of the question is looking for. Read the question carefully and then answer that question. You may find that all of the answers are true, but only one of them will actually answer the question that you are being asked. You need to make sure you focus on the question, not which answers are true or false.

There is only one right answer. Remember, there will only be one correct answer (unless the question specifically tells you otherwise). That means if you believe there is more than one right answer, you need to read the question and possibly the answers again. This will help you determine which one is the best possible answer to the question being asked.

Weed out wrong answers. If you come across a question that you don't know the answer to, take the time to read through the question carefully again and then read all of the answers. Does anything stand out to you? If it does, then that may be the correct answer. If you still don't know the answer, then read through and find one or two answers that are definitely false. You should be able to narrow down your options to fewer choices, which will give you a better chance of getting the right answer even if you have to guess.

Go back through. If you have some time at the end of the test, take that moment to go back through each question. Read through the question and the answer that you chose to make sure that it's correct. Make sure you're also checking that each question has an answer as well. You won't lose anything even if you have to guess, and you could end up helping yourself get more correct answers and points.

Circle/note essential words. If you have a paper test, you can circle words in the question that are most important in trying to answer that question. If you have a computer test, you can jot those words down so that when you look at the answers, you know what you're actually looking for. This helps you keep the focus on what's most important in the question and what kind of answer you need.

Restate the question. If you're not quite sure what the question is saying, try to read through it again and restate it in a different way. This will help you better understand what you're looking for when you start looking at the answers. You'll be able to easily see what you are looking for and get a better handle on how to work through the other questions as well.

If any part of a statement is false, then the entire statement is false. There is no such thing as 'half-true' on your exam. If you read the statement and you know that it is not accurate, then that is your answer. Do not second-guess yourself once you get to something that is false.

Watch for negative words. You may find yourself reading a question that refers to when you should 'not' do something or which of the following is 'not' true. If that's the case, make sure you're reading the answers correctly and answering the question based on that word. You don't want to answer the question based on a positive when it's asking for a negative.

Watch for definitive words. If you're reading a question or an answer and it uses words like 'always,' 'all,' 'none,' or 'never,' make sure you read through everything else on that question even more carefully. These sorts of definitive words are going to be a crucial part of getting the answer correct. Often these words will help you eliminate specific answers but not always.

Don't second-guess yourself without cause. If you think you know the answer to a question but then change your mind, it could be that you are actually realizing a better answer. On the other hand, you could be changing a correct answer to an incorrect one. Make sure that you can justify just why you are changing your answer and that there is a valid reason before you do.

Be prepared. We talked earlier about different ways that you can make sure that you are prepared for the test and what you need to do to get yourself ready. Go through all of those and make sure that you start long before you actually need to take the exam. This will help you feel confident walking into test day and will make sure you get more correct answers.

Get there early. You will need to make an appointment to take your test, so make sure you get there a little early, so you have a moment to relax and focus on what you're going to do. If you're taking the test online, make sure that you sit down a few minutes early and just breathe and focus on what you're going to be doing. This will help you to mentally prepare.

Compare answers. When you're looking for the best possible answer, don't be afraid to compare them to each other. This may be an excellent way to look at questions you aren't sure about once you get the answers narrowed down to two or three. You want to look at the question and then compare each of the answers to the question and to each other. You may be able to find the correct answer, or you may find another that you know is false.

Use other questions. You never know what kind of questions you will be asked on your test. It is possible that one of the other questions will actually give you the answer to the question that you're struggling with. Keep your eyes peeled as you work through each question for information that could help you to answer something else.

Don't get overwhelmed. It's easy to start feeling overwhelmed when you get into the middle of your test and aren't quite sure what you're doing or if you get to a question that you don't have any idea on. If that happens, it's essential to take a moment to sit back and breathe so you can relax and start again. You may want to skip over that question for now and come back to it later, so you don't get too worked up.

Practice relaxation techniques. You're likely to feel a little overwhelmed or a little anxious even when you first sit down for your test. Even though it's not an extended test, it is an important one, and you want to make sure that you're fully prepared and thinking at your best. The best way to do that is to make sure that you take a few deep breaths whenever you need to in order to reset and prepare yourself for the next question.

You don't have to be perfect. You do not have to get every single question correct in order to pass your test, and you don't need to worry about trying to do so either. Don't put too much pressure on yourself to get any specific score other than one that's high enough for you to pass the test.

Focus on the question in front of you. Don't think about the entire test while you're taking it. Instead, focus only on the question that's right in front of you at the moment. That's the only one that matters until it's answered. Then you move on to the next question, and you focus exclusively on that one until it's answered. Do this all the way through the test.

Let it go. If you aren't sure about a question after you've answered it, just mark it down to come back later and let it go. Move on to the next question. Focusing too much on any one question while you should be working on the next one is only going to stress you out. You'll find yourself struggling to get the next question right if you're overthinking about what you've missed or what you might have done wrong. Just let it go until it's time to come back.

Read the entire question. Don't skip over words or jump only to the last part of a question. Some questions might have additional information that you need to know before you can answer, or the additional information may help you choose the correct answer. You don't want to miss out on any kind of help because you jumped to the question specifically instead of reading the background.

Fill in the blanks right. If you have a fill-in-the-blank question, you will still be given answers to choose from. Remember that if there is more than one blank, all of the words in the selected answer must fit the blanks that are provided. If there are two blanks, for example, the first word in the answer must match the first blank, and the second word must fit the second blank. If both terms do not fit or do not fit in order, it is not the correct answer.

Watch the grammar. You aren't going to be scored based on grammar usage, but generally, if you look at the answer and the question, they will share the same grammatical structure. They will both be written in present tense or both in the past tense, for example. They might also use similar terms or vocabulary that can help you answer the question.

Look for opposite answers. When you read the answers, look for any that seem to be opposites. Both of these answers can't be correct, so you should be able to get rid of one. The other may be your right answer as well. Reread the question to see which one makes more sense.

Compare the answer to the question. When you've answered your question, make sure that you reread the answer and the question to make sure they match. Is your answer actually the answer to what's being asked, or did you choose a true statement that doesn't fit the question? You want to select the correct answer.

The question is always correct. If the question asks you about a specific situation, it doesn't matter if that situation is rare or unlikely. All of the information in the question, including information that is used to 'set the stage,' must be assumed to be correct. That means you should look at the question and believe everything that you are told and then answer the question based on that information.

Work out tricky words. If you've been studying the terminology and vocab for your test, you should be familiar with anything that you will come across on your test, but that's not always a guarantee. Make sure that if you do come across a word or term you don't know, you're reading the words around it, sounding it out, and breaking it down to try and understand as much as you can. You may even be able to work out what the question is asking by reading through the answers.

Eliminate answers that add information. Your answer should answer the question, but it likely won't add any extra information that wasn't in the scope of the question. If you have answers that seem to add more information, then they're likely not what you're looking for.

The longest answer isn't always the right one. Just because an answer is long and/or detailed, that doesn't mean that it's necessarily the correct answer. The same is true for an answer that is short and concise. That doesn't mean it's necessarily wrong or right. You should treat it just like you would any of the other answers and give it the same consideration.

Eliminate anything obviously wrong. In most cases, you can find at least one answer to the question which is obviously wrong. It will be completely irrelevant or factually inaccurate or won't even make sense. If that's the case, you can eliminate it as a possibility and immediately start looking at the other answers.

Avoid distractions. If you are taking the exam online at home or even at another testing facility, you want to make sure you avoid distractions. That means turning off phones or other devices that might make a lot of noise and keeping away from others who might interfere. If you're somewhere that others might interrupt, make sure you put a note on the door that you are not to be disturbed or let them know that you will come back out of the room when you are finished.

Ignore distractions. If you are at a testing center or if you are in a noisy place where you can't completely eliminate the distractions, you may need to work on ways to minimize them in your own mind. This might mean working on your own techniques to tune out sounds or to try and focus more carefully.

By taking a look at each of these tips and strategies for your test day, you will be better prepared to get things done and to answer your questions accurately. Remember, this is not a long test, and it's not designed to trick you. The information is all things you should know from your driver education course and/or reading through the Driver Handbook. Don't let yourself get too overwhelmed or worked up, and you should be just fine.

ANSWERS TO PRACTICE QUESTIONS

1. Middle or left lane
2. Hydroplaning
3. Between 15 and 50 feet
4. Driving on a well-lit road OR within 500 feet of an oncoming vehicle OR within 300 feet of a vehicle you're following
5. The push-pull technique (also called hand-to-hand)
6. Yield to vehicles on the right
7. One half hour before sunrise
8. 18 inches
9. You may cross the line to pass other vehicles
10. Pull over to the right edge of the road if possible
11. Slow down and proceed with caution
12. 100 feet
13. A solid yellow line

14. Your low-beam headlights
15. In a crosswalk, on a sidewalk, and within an intersection
16. On the right side of the island
17. .08%
18. Keep your vehicle moving straight
19. Down to the lower right side of your lane
20. The driver and all passengers
21. When the pavement markings prohibit it, when there are two or more traffic lanes in each direction, when you're within 100 feet of an intersection
22. Shift into a lower gear
23. 240 feet
24. Stop
25. 30 mph
26. Shifting your eyes frequently
27. Four seconds
28. Large flashing or sequencing arrow panels
29. Blind Spots
30. Yellow lines
31. If the vehicle is making or about to make a left turn OR if the vehicle is slowing, stopped, or disabled on the main traveled portion of the roadway
32. Yield to vehicles already on the main road
33. Keep right
34. White
35. Broken yellow line

36. Middle lanes
37. From a one-way street onto another one-way street
38. Tailgating
39. You must obey the flag persons results
40. Neck injuries if you are hit from behind
41. Keeping to the far side of your lane and reducing your speed slightly
42. Increase your speed
43. Follow the flag persons signals no matter which lane are you in
44. Increase your speed
45. Come to a complete stop and then yield the right-of-way to pedestrians, bicyclists, and vehicles on the road you are entering
46. Not permitted in either direction
47. Leftmost
48. Longer distances to slow down than cars
49. Hazard flashers
50. As close as possible to the speed of traffic
51. Stop your vehicle if necessary
52. Set the parking brake, stop the engine, and remove the ignition key
53. Move into an acceleration lane
54. Left hand and arm straight out, keeping hand and arm still
55. Left-right-left rule
56. Hand and arm extended upward

57. On the shoulder
58. Check your mirror and look over your shoulder toward the rear
59. Signal a left turn and look over your left shoulder
60. A work zone sign
61. Increase your following distance
62. 10 Seconds
63. Safety belt
64. Hold the steering wheel tightly and keep your vehicle going straight
65. All traffic coming into the opposite direction
66. Indicate your intention by signaling, look in your mirrors, look over your shoulder
67. The vehicle traveling uphill
68. The middle or left lanes
69. Quickly tap your brake pedal three to four times
70. You may cross the line to pass other vehicles
71. Turning traffic must stop
72. Pull over to the right side of the road
73. Slow down and let the vehicle pass first
74. Four times
75. Spotting hazards well in advance
76. A counterclockwise
77. Stop
78. Stop before the line
79. Make it on a curve in the road or near a hill without sufficient visibility

80. Following too closely
81. Slow down or stop
82. Turn the steering wheel in the direction of the skid
83. A sideswipe accident
84. Follow too closely
85. Warning signs
86. The yellow arrow is about to change red
87. Stop if it is safe to do so
88. Slow down and stop if necessary
89. Oil in the asphalt
90. Steer right toward the shoulder or curb line
91. A three-point turn
92. 180 days
93. $1,000
94. The left edge of the pavement
95. Moved into a non-adjacent lane if possible; otherwise slow down
96. Faster tire wear
97. On roadways with at least two lanes traveling in your direction, on one-way streets, where all lanes of traffic are moving in the same direction, when the vehicle is in a left-turn lane
98. One year
99. $2,000
100. Six days
101. 90 days
102. 30 days

103. Two years
104. Railroad crossing ahead
105. Hospital ahead
106. Road surface higher than shoulder surface
107. Bump ahead
108. Steep hill ahead
109. Turn left or go straight
110. Airport ahead
111. Keep to the right of the traffic island
112. No trucks allowed
113. Stop sign ahead
114. U-turn only on indicated lane
115. Slow moving vehicle
116. U-turn allowed
117. Livestock crossing
118. Road ends, turn left or right
119. Lodging facilities ahead
120. Left turn only
121. Railroad crossing here
122. Flag person ahead
123. No left turns allowed
124. Speed limit 40 mph
125. Passing allowed across lanes in same direction of traffic
126. Right side of roadway, one-way road
127. Left side of roadway, one-way road
128. Shoulder is hazardous, do not leave pavement
129. Center lane left turns for both directions of traffic

130. Incoming merging traffic
131. Upcoming side road
132. Public phones ahead
133. Curves ahead in roadway
134. Roundabout ahead
135. Right turns not allowed
136. Pedestrian crossing ahead
137. HOV (carpool) lane ahead
138. Divided highway ends
139. Roadway turns right
140. Do not enter
141. Road entering a curve ahead
142. No bicycles allowed
143. Beginning of an alternate road ahead
144. Narrow bridge ahead
145. Bicycle crossing ahead
146. Divided highway ends
147. Series of curves ahead
148. Take turns more slowly
149. Slow down when approaching animals that are standing near the road, look well down the road and far off to each side, scan the sides of the road to watch for the reflection of vehicle headlights in the eyes of animals
150. Advising sign for appropriate ramp speed at exit
151. Sudden stops, driving slower than the normal flow of traffic, weaving between lanes

152. Pull off the road and park your vehicle. Turn off the ignition, get away from the car, and call the Fire Department
153. They are hard to see in traffic
154. To keep a smooth traffic flow
155. Keep your eyes moving, stay alert, be ready to react to road hazards
156. Diamond
157. You cannot see without moving your head
158. The right lane
159. If traffic conditions require it
160. Makes you less aware of what is happening to your driving abilities
161. Stop
162. Traffic signals ahead
163. Mirrors leave "blind spots" behind both sides of vehicles
164. Pass red lights, go the wrong way, exceed the speed limit
165. Be prepared to stop for the red light
166. Signal your turn, check for bicyclists and pedestrians, and do not turn directly in front of a bicyclist or pedestrians
167. Signal, check your mirrors and blind spot in the direction you plan to move, and then change lanes
168. Wear approved helmets
169. Stop before the intersection

170. Makes it difficult for drivers to judge their condition, increases reaction time, makes drivers more prone to take chances
171. Broken white
172. Slippery when wet
173. Increase the following distance
174. To reduce your speed
175. Illegal to possess an open container of alcohol in the passenger compartment
176. Yes
177. Road ahead has a sharp right turn followed by a sharp left turn
178. Do not stop for any reason, keep moving until you can safely pull off the road
179. Hand signals
180. .02% or higher
181. The driver on the left must yield to the driver on the right
182. Divided highway ahead, stay to the right
183. Watch for this species crossing the road
184. Turn on your emergency flashers and leave your low beams on
185. Intersection ahead
186. Green; white
187. Get out of the car and check behind the car
188. Pedestrians should finish crossing the street if started
189. Move as far away from traffic as possible

190. Detour to the right
191. Flash your headlights to high beam for a second and then return to low beam
192. Come to a complete stop
193. Time
194. Stay in the driver's seat with both hands clearly in sight on the steering wheel
195. Two-way traffic
196. Yield to intersecting traffic, prepare to stop
197. No U-turns allowed
198. Ease your foot off the gas pedal and brake gently
199. One hour
200. Ride side-by-side in a single lane
201. Move into the right lane and allow other vehicles to pass you on the left
202. Look toward the right side of the road
203. Arrange to ride home with a friend who does not drink
204. Reduce
205. Their lane has a solid yellow center line, they approach a curve on a two-way road and cannot see around it, they cannot safely return to the right lane before any oncoming vehicle comes within 200 feet of them
206. Slow down before entering the curve
207. Approach the turn in the left lane or from the left side of a single lane
208. Only when necessary, to avoid collisions

209. Must stop and yield the right-of-way to traffic on the roadway and to pedestrians
210. Take longer than cars to stop
211. Look for a detour or another route
212. When making turns
213. Be prepared to stop before the intersection
214. Take your attention away from driving, take your hands off the wheel, take your eyes off the road
215. Where there is a red light, when a traffic officer orders them to stop, at an intersection with a stop sign
216. Drive with the flow of traffic
217. Prepare to leave the lane safely
218. Stop and wait for a large gap in traffic and then enter the highway and accelerate quickly
219. Passing is permitted on the side of the broken yellow line
220. Stop
221. Press your brakes in slow, steady strokes
222. The road surface ahead changes to a low-type surface or earth road
223. Center lane is shared for left turns
224. Arrows
225. Are slowing down or stopping
226. Diamond shaped
227. Give information about directions and distances
228. Provides advanced notice of upcoming speed limit change

229. Avoid driving on either side of the truck and don't tailgate
230. Wait until the vehicles clear the intersection before entering
231. The pedestrian has the right of way
232. Driving as near to the right edge of the road as possible and stopping
233. Stop and not turn under any circumstances
234. You are approaching from behind
235. Is the reason for most rear-end collisions
236. Let the call go to voicemail
237. Left, right, and left again
238. Avoid making fast turns and stops
239. Toward the right edge of your lane
240. Drive slowly enough so you can stop within an area lighted by your headlights
241. Others involved in the collision
242. Wait until the person crosses the street
243. Look over your right shoulder through your rear window
244. May cross the lines to turn left into a private driveway
245. See the vehicle or vehicles headlights in your rearview mirror
246. The road is closed to traffic in your direction
247. Away from the curb
248. Your car has broken down on the roadway
249. Slowly ease your foot off the gas pedal

250. Need a large enough gap to get up to the speed of traffic
251. Their smaller size makes them harder to see
252. Be prepared for workers and equipment ahead
253. Same
254. Look for passive vehicles, bicyclists, and motorcyclists
255. Cannot see the truck driver in the truck's side mirrors
256. Stop before entering
257. Required to use both the lap and shoulder belts
258. Stop and let the pedestrian finish crossing
259. They tend to freeze before the rest of the road does
260. Right towards the side of the road
261. You have the right-of-way
262. Lane ends or roadway narrows ahead
263. Two seconds
264. Slow down and very carefully turn back onto the pavement
265. Your full name and address and reasonable assistance to anyone who has been injured
266. Octagon
267. You may not have time to stop if the vehicle in front of you slows or stops suddenly
268. Four seconds
269. Get off at the next exit and come back to the exit you missed
270. Always keep their eyes moving, look for developing trouble spots, have plans of action

271. Follow the directions given by the officer
272. Changing lanes, pulling into or out of a parking space, pulling into traffic from a parking area or alley
273. Bicyclists
274. Swing too wide for your lane
275. Dangerous
276. Visibility is reduced in the dark
277. On an incline
278. Look both ways before crossing tracks, pay attention, and obey all traffic signals
279. Under no circumstance
280. Allow extra time for your trip
281. 15 mph
282. Slow down and wait until there is no traffic approaching and then pass the bicyclist while leaving them sufficient space
283. Don't stop for any reason. Keep moving until you can safely pull off the road
284. 20 feet
285. Parking spaces are reserved for people with disabled parking permits
286. You must bear either right or left
287. Never
288. Follow the directions given by the crossing guard
289. When driving in fog, dust, or rain, when following closely behind another vehicle at night, within 500 feet of an approaching vehicle when driving at night

290. Be sure all the occupants of the vehicle have buckled their seatbelts
291. Pedestrians
292. Shift to neutral and apply steady pressure on the brake
293. Can be ticketed
294. The maximum speed limit, a speed that is faster than is reasonable and prudent, or a speed that is safe for existing conditions
295. May create a dangerous driving environment
296. It is against the law to go around lowered gates at a crossing, you must stop at a railroad crossing when directed to do so by a flagger, not all railroad crossings are equipped with flashing red signals and gates
297. Once every year
298. A serious traffic safety problem
299. The maximum legal speed on the roadway is 55 mph
300. Yellow
301. A privilege
302. Time
303. Turn on your headlights
304. Check for traffic, pedestrians, and bicyclists before moving forward
305. Workers are on or very close to the road in the work zone ahead
306. Stop and let the pedestrian cross
307. Drivers in the proper lane must make the movement

indicated by the arrow while following directions indicated by traffic signals

308. To stop, to change lanes, or for unexpected movement from works or equipment
309. Your reflexes and reaction time slow down, your judgement of speed and distance is distorted, you are less alert
310. Yield the right-of-way to pedestrians
311. Inattentive driving, excessive speed under the driving conditions, following other vehicles too closely
312. 50 feet
313. 500 feet
314. Wait until you can see both headlights of the passed car in your rearview mirror before returning to your original lane
315. Signal at least 100 feet before changing lanes to pass and ensure there is no oncoming traffic
316. A flashing or solid red light
317. To avoid conflict with other traffic
318. Usually causes the driver to react more slowly to hazards
319. Doubled
320. Stop immediately, help the injured, and call the police
321. Should yield the right-of-way to cross traffic
322. You are able to clearly see the road ahead, you can return to your lane before meeting oncoming traffic,

and your vehicle is capable of the speed necessary to pass
323. White
324. Have the right-of-way when using sirens, horns, or lights, may use a loudspeaker to give instructions, and may follow each other
325. Not move the injured unnecessarily. Keep the injured warm and administer first aid
326. Keep your windshield and mirror clear, allow additional distance between your vehicle and the vehicles that you are following, and approach all vehicles with caution
327. Drivers should come to a complete stop and proceed if the crosswalk is clear
328. Will result in license suspension
329. Sound your horn
330. Slow down and proceed with caution
331. Is buckled snugly across your hip bones and lower abdomen
332. The effect that alcohol has
333. Your seat
334. For the first 10 to 15 minutes of a rainstorm
335. Slow down gradually while checking their rearview mirror, move into the left lane, and watch for oncoming vehicles and pedestrians
336. Look around the vehicle for children and obstructing objects, signal to other drivers, and check their mirrors

337. Turn into the lane that will interfere the least with traffic
338. The bridge ahead may be too narrow to meet or pass a truck
339. Drivers may drive normally in this lane
340. Never enter a street or crosswalk when vehicles are approaching
341. Should yield to drivers already on the public road
342. In the direction you want the vehicle to go
343. Drivers may proceed with caution
344. Use your side and rearview mirrors and check your blind spots, use the acceleration lane to adjust your speed to match the speed of freeway traffic, and yield to traffic already on the freeway
345. Moving more slowly
346. In designated litter barrels
347. Drivers should merge into the lane indicated by the arrow
348. Drive with the flow of traffic
349. 30 feet
350. Wear your seatbelt
351. Be ready to stop for any train that may appear
352. When you can see the passed vehicle in your rearview mirror
353. A stop sign
354. Accelerate to the speed of traffic
355. Stop and look for a train

356. That an action is forbidden
357. When you see a flashing red or blue light or hear a siren
358. Never
359. Be prepared to stop if a train is nearby
360. A triangular orange sign
361. Turn off the engine, lock the ignition and remove the key, and set the parking brake
362. Vacate the lane closest to the emergency vehicle or slow down
363. Extremely dangerous
364. Has the same meaning as a circular red traffic light for that lane or direction of travel
365. At intersections and pedestrian crosswalks
366. Assume the driver cannot see you and may open their door
367. Pay attention to their surroundings, follow instructions, and reduce their speed at least to the posted advisory speed
368. Never
369. 29%
370. Move forward or drop back so the other driver can see you
371. Drivers may pass if it is safe to do so
372. Turn right
373. When pedestrians are in crosswalks, they should be given the right-of-way

374. The signal is about to change to a red X
375. Under no circumstances
376. Yield to oncoming vehicles
377. The road is curving sharply to the left
378. Slow down and be prepared to stop if necessary
379. Prepare to yield to any train at the crossing
380. 70 mph
381. Less than ideal conditions are present for driving
382. Do not make any sudden changes in speed or direction
383. Lanes are moving in opposite directions and drivers are not permitted to pass
384. Reduce their speed and increase their following distance
385. Your vehicle has two or more occupants
386. Must exit the freeway, if you stay in your current lane
387. 15 mph
388. Take a few minutes to cool off before you begin your drive home
389. Is a good driving habit and is required by law
390. Move to another lane, if safe, to let traffic enter
391. Decrease your speed
392. Be sure the passing lane is clear
393. Black letters or symbols on a yellow background
394. Side of the road facing oncoming traffic
395. If their current location is a danger to themselves or others
396. Broken white or yellow

397. Should stop where they have a clear view of approaching traffic before they enter the intersecting roadway
398. Provide information for drivers

8

DRIVING TEST STRATEGIES

When it comes to preparing for the Texas driver's license test, some people feel more nervous about the written test portion, while others feel more anxious about the driving portion. We've already taken a look at the written part of the exam and how you can best prepare. We've also taken a look at many of the questions that you might see on the exam and the answers that you need to know. We're now going to take a little time to go over how you can prepare yourself for the driving portion of the test.

This portion of the test is just as significant as your written portion, but you may not feel like you have to worry about it as much. After all, you are required to practice driving in order to even apply for your driver's license. And you'll have spent some time driving while you were working on your permit as well. But keep in mind that your actual driving test isn't like driving with your parent or other licensed adult. You will need to practice specific things.

Review the 'How to Prepare for a Drive Test' flyer from the Department of Public Safety. This document is going to lay out everything that you need to know about the driving test. It's actually relatively short and will give you a checklist of everything that you need to do and know in order to do well on the driving portion of your test.

Make sure your vehicle will pass inspection. In order to take your car out, you will need to make sure it passes inspection. The instructor who will be going with you for the road test will look over the vehicle and check that it meets all requirements. All vehicles in Texas must undergo this inspection each year, so this should not be anything different, and the car should be able to pass inspection if it has been on the road previously.

Take a deep breath. This is an important test, and you want to make sure that you're going to pass, but you absolutely need to relax, or you're not going to be able to. That means taking a breath before you get started and running through the list of things you need to do in your head. This will help you get prepared and will make sure that you can feel more confident when it comes time to pull out on the road.

Review vehicle controls. You should make sure that you know how to operate everything in the vehicle that you are going to take to your exam. If this is not the vehicle that you usually use for practice driving, take a little time to familiarize yourself with where the shifter is, how the pedals feel, where the turn signals are, and more. You should also know how to turn on the windshield wipers and headlights.

Wear your seatbelt. You are required by law to wear your seatbelt while in the vehicle. Make sure that you put yours on immediately after getting into the car. If you attempt to drive without first putting on your seatbelt, your instructor may give you a failing grade immediately for unsafe behavior, and you may be required to take your test again another day. Make sure you have the seatbelt on properly and buckled securely.

Practice with the car you will drive on test day. Even if you usually drive a different vehicle for your practice, you should take the car you will be driving on test day out at least a few times. This will help you get more comfortable with the way that it drives and the way it feels while you're going through each of the motions that you need to do when you're on your test. You want to feel comfortable, and if you're driving a vehicle for the first time, that will be unlikely.

Do a practice run. When you practice driving with anyone, it's not the same as taking your driving test. Have someone take you out and do a mock driving test rather than just practicing by driving to the store or a friend's house. This will give you a little more of the experience and help you practice things in a way similar to what you will be asked on test day.

Write down questions beforehand. Before you get to the DPS, you'll want to write down any questions or concerns that you have about the driving test. Remember, you will have an opportunity to ask these questions before the test begins but not after. Don't make the mistake of assuming you will remember your questions only to start the test before you do. The person driving with you is not able to answer your questions at that time.

Ask your questions. You will need to ask any necessary questions before you get in the vehicle to start your driving test. Once you get in the car, and the test begins, the instructor will not be allowed to answer questions for you. They will only be able to give you instructions on what you need to do, and it will be up to you to execute those. That means you should make sure you are clear on what's going to happen before this point.

Practice defensive driving. Defensive driving means that you are aware of what other people are doing at all times and that you are paying attention when they make sudden movements. This allows you to react more quickly and helps you to avoid getting into an accident. Driving defensively is an essential process on your driving test and otherwise and can help you do better on your test.

Drive smoothly. This means both speeding up and slowing down, making turns, changing lanes, stopping at lights and signs, and even approaching intersections. You want to make sure that you are going through all of these motions as smoothly as possible and avoiding jerking or shuddering. This will definitely show that you are a more experienced driver and makes it more likely you will get a better review.

Follow posted signs. Any posted signs that you come across should be followed, especially when you are on your driving test but otherwise as well. This means making sure you do not exceed speed limits, that you yield to others at intersections, and more. If the conditions are not ideal, you may want to drive slower than the speed limit in order to show that you are safety-conscious.

Stay back from other vehicles. Don't get too close to other cars while you are taking your driving test. Remember that you should be two seconds behind in ideal weather conditions and more when the weather is not perfect or if there is a great deal of traffic. This allows you to have a safe stopping distance if the vehicle in front of you were to slam on their brakes out of nowhere.

Stay in your lane. Know which lane you should be in at all times, and then make sure that you are in it. If you need to change lanes, make sure you know which lane you should change to and that you do so as smoothly as possible. This will help you follow traffic and follow the instructions your driving instructor gives you.

Use proper signals. Be sure that you are using any signals necessary when you are turning or changing lanes. Also, make sure that you use your signals 100 feet before you will be making the move. You may be asked about hand signals while you are driving. Make sure you know what the proper hand signals are for any turns or movements you need to make so you can answer the questions.

Make movements visible. When you check your mirrors or look behind you before a turn or lane change, you may not always do so with large movements. When you are taking a driving test, however, you will need to be careful about the movements that you make and be sure that you turn your head so that the instructor can see you are checking. They may not be able to recognize you checking mirrors if you aren't doing this.

Watch traffic. You should do this by looking around you frequently, not just when you're changing lanes, turning, or approaching an intersection. You should also make sure that you check your mirrors and physically look out your windows. This will help you keep a better eye on what's happening around you and if sudden movements are needed.

Keep both hands on the wheel. Even if you usually drive with only one hand on the wheel, you should keep both hands on the wheel when you are taking your driving test. This will look better to the instructor and will make you safer as well. In fact, your instructor may consider driving without both hands on the wheel to be a dangerous activity.

React quickly but carefully. If something happens or if you are asked to do something, make sure that you are reacting swiftly but that you are still careful about the maneuver that you need to make. If there is an emergency situation, you may need to respond quickly to what is around you. Make sure you do so in whatever way you safely can for yourself, the instructor, and anyone else around you.

Watch your blind spots. Look over your shoulder periodically or check the blind spots in your vehicle in any way that you can. You need to do this if you are turning or changing lanes, but you should also do it occasionally otherwise so that you don't miss a vehicle that is acting in a hazardous fashion or could pose a danger to you. Make sure you can do this without moving the car in the lane.

Know your blind spots. In order to watch the blind spots in your vehicle, you have to know precisely where they are. This is important for each car that you get into. You should always be aware of where the blind spots are and how you can compensate for them, whether it means moving the mirrors or turning your head or body to see.

You will be asked to perform several different maneuvers while driving your vehicle. Make sure that you are comfortable executing each of them while in the car that you take to your test.

- Backing in a straight line. You should be able to put your vehicle into reverse and back up in a straight line. This means you need to keep the wheel straight, and you need to keep an eye on what's behind you, so you don't back into anything.
- Parallel parking. This can be a difficult one for many people, but you need to be able to execute it properly, bringing your car into the middle of the parking spot and without hitting cones or other obstacles around you. This involves pulling up to the side of a vehicle and backing correctly into the space behind it, as well as making sure your car is straight and fully in the space.
- Approaching intersections. You should know how to act or what to do depending on whether the intersection you are approaching has a stop sign or yield sign or what color the light is that you are approaching. Remember that a yellow light means that you should stop and wait for the light to cycle again. You should always slow slightly when approaching an intersection to allow adequate time for any reaction that you need to make.
- Turning. Turning in both directions is an essential part of your driving test. You need to be able to turn alongside traffic as well as across traffic. You should also practice turning from a stopped position or not, turning with a light, or timing your turn between

vehicles. You never know which of these ways you will be asked to execute a turn when it comes to your driving test.

- Stopping in regular traffic conditions. You need to be able to stop your vehicle reasonably when required. For your driving test, you will be required to stop your car at stop signs or lights. You may be asked to stop otherwise while driving if it is safe to do so and will need to show that you can do so without jerking or jarring the vehicle or your passengers.

- Controlling the vehicle. You must be in complete control of your car at all times. Even if the conditions are not ideal, you need to be able to drive smoothly and at a reasonable speed as well as executing any other maneuvers you need, such as stopping and taking off, turning, changing lanes, and more. All of these things must be done without the vehicle sliding or skidding, even in rough weather.

- Observing traffic. You need to be aware of what is happening around you at all times. There could be any number of other vehicles on the road, and you never know what they may or may not be doing. That's why it's crucial for you to be able to watch those vehicles and react as necessary to their actions. Be aware of cars all the way around you as well as those approaching or even moving away.

- Maintaining vehicle position. Whatever you're

supposed to be doing, you should be able to do it reasonably easily. You should be able to turn your vehicle safely and while staying in your designated lane. You should be able to stop the car where it needs to be, behind the crosswalk, and you should be able to keep pace with the vehicles around you without getting too close. These methods of maintaining vehicle position and more will be vital for your test.
- Using signals. Always make sure that you signal when you are changing lanes or when you are turning. You should be doing this 100 feet out but make sure you turn them on as soon as possible if you happen to forget. If you are closer than 100 feet, you may lose points for your score, but you will not lose as many as if you fail to signal at all. This could even be an automatic failure if you do not use a signal at all.

Avoid dangerous/illegal behaviors. If you engage in any behavior that is considered dangerous or illegal, your test will immediately be stopped. You will be required to immediately return to the DPS office where you started, and you will receive a failing result on your test. There are many different situations that could be considered dangerous, so make sure that you are driving safely and defensively to avoid any of these behaviors. Illegal behaviors should be easily recognized.

Know your result. When the test is done, you're going to know whether you passed or failed immediately. Make sure you know what your result is, and then do what needs to be done afterward. If you have passed, you will be able to take your result and get your driver's license. (Or at least get the temporary driver's license until yours comes in the mail.) If you did not, you will need to take some time to practice and take the test again.

Don't wait too long. Don't wait around too long to take your driver's test the first time or any subsequent times if you don't pass the first time. The first time you should be preparing but taking your test once you've spent a reasonable amount of time studying and practicing. If you don't pass the first time, your application is valid for 90 days or three attempts at the test. After that, you will need to apply and pay the fee again.

Find out what happened. If possible, ask the person who did the road test with you about what happened and why you did not pass. This is not the time to negotiate or try to get them to change their decision. This is a time to learn what you need to practice so that you can do better the next time and get a passing score. If they know that you are not trying to get them to change their answer, the instructor may be more willing to give you tips and advice.

Get more practice. If you don't pass your driving test the first time around, don't get discouraged. It's time to just dust yourself off and get a little more practice so that you can try again. You will want to practice anything that you were told you didn't do well on, as well as general driving tips again, so you don't miss something different the next time around. You want to make sure you can pass the second time you take the test.

Get a professional to help. You may want to practice with your parent or guardian or the licensed driver that you have been driving with. You may also want to work with a driving instructor to get a better idea of how you did on the test and how you're likely to do the next time. They can go over your driving process with you in a similar way as the instructor with whom you took your test to help you.

Taking the driving test is going to be a bit nerve-wracking (or maybe quite nerve-wracking). You're going to be a little overwhelmed or nervous when you walk in, and you may feel nervous when you get out on the road. Don't let your nerves get the better of you. This is something that you've practiced and worked hard for, and you know what you're doing even if it doesn't feel like it at the moment. Take the time to focus and pay attention to what you're doing and what's being asked of you, and you're going to do just fine.

9

ADDITIONAL RESOURCES

This book's content should help you get where you need to be to pass both the knowledge and the skills portions of your driver's license test. But if you feel like you're going to need a little more help, we've put together a host of additional resources that you can check out. We have a list of different books and websites that you can look at for more information. We've also put together a list of places where you can take pre-tests and even some of the government sites, pages, and more that you should check out.

Looking at each of these will help you get a better idea of what you need to know and will help you feel more prepared when it comes to taking your test. That doesn't mean you need to use all of these resources. Instead, look through them and see which ones are the best option for you or for the areas where you seem to be struggling and opt for those areas. Or you could choose to look at free options and then go to paid options if you need them later. For now, let's take a look at what's out there.

Books

If you learn well from books, you may want to take a look at any of these options to help you out. Some are available in physical copies (if you prefer that option), and others are strictly eBooks. Either way, you can learn a lot of information related to the driving test and the knowledge exam that you will need to take in Texas. If you decide to look for additional books for yourself to supplement these, keep in mind that the Texas exams will be different from those in other states, and make sure you get the right options.

The Driving Book: Everything New Drivers Need to Know But Don't Know to Ask by Karen Gravelle

This book is intended to help you learn more about passing your driving test, including things that you may never have even thought about. In fact, this book not only talks about how to pass your test but also focuses on some of the things that you may face after you get your license, like caring for the car and negotiating driving privileges and lousy weather. It's a short book that's good for those who are just getting through driver's training courses or who are early in their studying for the driver's license process.

Texas Driver Handbook by the Department of Public Safety

This is one book that you absolutely need to read from beginning to end. It's actually produced by the Department of Public Safety, and you should be going through it as part of your driver's education program, but either way, you should be reading it for yourself as well. By taking the time to do so, you'll learn all the rules and regulations that are going to be on your driver's test, as well as the things you'll be asked to do when it comes to actually driving.

2020 Drivers Manual for Texas: Everything New Drivers Need to Know by Jesse Cole

This book is updated for the new year and includes everything you should need in order to prepare for the test that you're going to take. It's going to give you a total of 300 different questions and answers, which can help you feel more confident going into the exam, and it's geared toward beginners, so you will find out anything and everything you need to know.

Texas DMV Test Manual by Donald Frias

You'll get a total of 300 different questions and answers included in this book, which will help you prepare for the license test. The goal is to make sure that you can pass the test the first time that you sit for it, so reading through this book should help you learn about different things like defensive driving, traffic control, special driving conditions, and road signs.

Texas DMV for Driving License Permit by Wince N. George

Getting your license or even getting your permit is going to require you to do some research and some studying. This book is designed to help you get all the information that you need and includes 200 questions and answers to help you feel more confident. It's designed to work alongside the driver's manual that we already mentioned, so you have a strong foundation of knowledge for the final exam.

Texas DMV Permit Practice Test Manual by Diana S. Hill

When it comes to the written exam, it seems that this is the hardest part for most to master. Even if you think you know the material, it can be hard to answer the questions in the moment. This book offers plenty of practice questions with answers as well as the information that you will need to do well on them. It focuses on each of the crucial areas where you may be tested for your driver's license exam.

2020 Texas DMV Permit Test Questions by Edward W. Johnson

This book will help you get through the latest version of the DMV test so that you can get your driver's license. It's geared toward the written exam, but the information in it can also help you with the driving exam. You'll get over 200 test questions and answers that will help you understand the laws and rules of the road as well as common traffic signs and symbols, so you're more comfortable going into both parts of your test.

Drive Right: You Are the Driver by Prentice Hall

This book is more general and geared toward drivers from all different states and shouldn't be used alone as you need focused attention on the laws and regulations in your state. This can help you better understand signs and other aspects of driving and the exam that will be common across the country, which will allow you to prepare alongside reading through other books or your state's driving handbook.

Traffic: Why We Drive the Way We Do by Tom Vanderbilt

This book might not be so much about how to drive or even how to pass your written exam, but it's definitely going to be an excellent option to read and understand more about driving in general. Understanding some of the different aspects that go into driving and even some of the situations that you may find yourself in will make you a better driver and help you to be more successful on the road.

Pre-Tests

Next, we're going to talk about some places that you can take official pre-tests for the Texas license exam. These pre-tests are designed to present you with a set number of questions that are very similar to what you will find on the actual exam. You'll also be taking them all at once and won't be able to see the answers until you are finished. These types of pre-tests are good to help you gauge where you are right now as well as where you need to do additional work to improve your score before the official exam.

Driving Tests Texas

With this page, you'll be able to check out driving exams for any type of driving test in Texas. You can look at motorcycle tests, CDL tests, and car tests, as well as checking out handbooks and frequently asked questions for the Texas DMV. You can check out the diagnostic test to gauge where you are already and then try out three different practice tests entirely free. After that, you have to pay for additional tests but keep in mind each practice test is focused on a different area of the exam, which means you may want to look at taking as many as possible.

Texas Drivers Ed

This page offers you two completely free tests that might be short but will give you a good overview of what you need to know. This can help you get a good understanding of the information you'll see on the test, including different situations and even different signs that you might see. You'll be asked about different laws and rules of the road as well. There's even a separate warning signs test that you can take for free. All of the tests provide you with a score as well as correct answers when you're done.

DMV Written Test

Contrary to what it says, this website is not actually associated with the DMV, but it does offer you a practice driving exam with 30 questions. In fact, there are 24 different tests available, so you can try it out multiple times. Even better, everything is free, so you don't have to worry about paying for another option. You'll be able to pass the knowledge test with 70% or higher, and that's exactly what this test is going to give you as well. You'll even get scores for each page as you go along.

DMV Permit Test

If you're looking for a little bit of help and guidance, you can use the practice test available here. If you want even more assistance, they also have a premium option that gives you even more content and actually offers you a pass guarantee. Whether you're taking the regular driving test, the practice permit test, or a motorcycle test, you can get the information that you need with either of these options. It offers information that's designed to make sure you know everything that could possibly be included on your test.

Drivers Ed Hub

On this website, you'll find practice tests that will help you study for any of the vehicle driving tests that are associated with the Texas DMV. You can also choose a simulation test for the permit test, individual topic questions, or a DMV marathon test. Each of these is designed to help you understand what you might see on the actual exam. The simulation test is different each time, while the marathon test includes all of the questions available through this website.

Drivers Ed

Here you will find several tests that you can purchase to practice for the Texas exam as a teen. There are up to 50 tests available that you can buy individually or in sets, so you get as much content as you want. They also guarantee that you will pass the exam, or you can get the money you spent on those practice tests back. That can definitely make it a better investment and help you feel more confident. You can come back and log into your account to take the exams you purchase whenever you choose.

Virtual Drive

If you're looking for more support, you can take this State of Texas approved course, which gives you six hours of online training and support to help you with your test. You'll get immediate access to your certification, and you'll get a final test to take online. This process is going to make sure you know what you're doing, and it actually includes the official written driver test, so you don't have to make an appointment with the DPS (Department of Public Safety).

Test Guide

With this test guide page, you'll get several different practice tests for the Texas permit. In fact, there are four different practice tests that are completely free and a separate road signs test that's also free. If you're looking for more information, you can check out the frequently asked questions section, or you can purchase cheat sheets that are guaranteed to help you pass the exam. There are also plenty of other resources and links to help you find your local DPS office.

Free DMV Practice Tests

If you want to get some practice for any of the different DPS practice tests in Texas, you can do so here. You'll find a permit practice exam, a Full License practice exam, and one each for CDL endorsement and motorcycle permits. You'll also find a separate practice test that will help you with road signs and signals so you can feel more comfortable with this portion of both your road test and the written test.

Websites

Sometimes you don't need a full practice test or even a book to help you prepare. Sometimes just getting online and doing a bit of research for yourself is an excellent way to go. That's where these pages are going to help you. There's a whole lot of information here that will help you understand some of the different information you need to know in order to be successful on your driving test.

Texas Department of Licensing & Regulation

If you're looking for official information related to your driving exam or anything else in Texas, you may want to take a closer look at the official site of the Department of Licensing & Regulation. You can find out about the sign language driver education course, locate textbooks to help you pass, and even get information about your certificate form and different schools.

Texas Driving School

On this website, you're going to find a little bit of everything, including information for teen and adult applicants and information about different tests, courses, and more. There are even plenty about defensive driving and frequently asked questions. You can go through the entire driver education course here, whether you're a teen or an adult, or you can go through the defensive driving course to clear traffic tickets and more.

Driving School of North Texas

Here you'll find the Texas Handbook as well as all the information you need to pass your driving test. Not only that, but you'll find the course you need to take in order to do it. This website offers questions, state laws and policies, and information about how to prepare for your driving test. It also offers a log to keep track of the hours that you need to practice driving in order to apply for your license.

I Drive Safely

You can check out a resource guide directly for parents and teens that will help with a parent-led driver education program. It gives you full transparency, and everything is done online, so you can work through it whenever it's convenient for you. Not only that, but it's approved by the Texas DPS and offers a written exam, so you don't have to go through the DPS in order to get this taken care of.

Drivers Ed

There's a 100% pass rate and a guarantee when you take your test and your course through this website. That means you're going to pay for the process, but you don't need to worry about if you'll get through. It's also entirely online. If you need assistance for in-car driving lessons, defensive driving, and more, you can take care of all of that through the same website, which gives you all the information you need.

Texas Driving School

This company is rated an "A" with the BBB, which means you're working with someone who has a stellar record. They also have support 24/7 and provide you with all of the information you need to get through driver's ed without the lectures and the classroom experience. It's legal and meets all state requirements and comes in different versions for defensive driving and the driver's ed you need for your license.

All Ages Driving School

You can find information for just about everything related to the DPS here as well as information to help you with your test. That includes your permit documents, verification forms, right-of-way rules, workbooks, and questions. You'll also find a final exam review that can help you to prepare. If you're ready to take the course, you can do it online or check out locations and schedules for in-person classes.

Texas Adult Drivers Education

Those who are over the age of 18 but not quite 25 can take this course to get their certification. It's an inexpensive option and gives you all the resources that you need. You'll also get more information about scheduling driving lessons, completing the Impact portion of your driving requirements, and even more about how to get the test for those over 25 who don't need to take the driver's education course.

Pioneer Drivers Education School

There are all kinds of information here for teens and adults, including online classes, forms you'll need to go to the DPS, and even links to other information like the Impact video and the Texas Driver Handbook. You can check out water safety, practice tests, and even the ways that drugs and alcohol can impair driving, so you're ready for your exam.

DPS Information

When it comes to preparing for your driving test or the knowledge portion of your test, you definitely can't underestimate the importance of government websites. After all, you want to make sure that you're getting all of your information from a reliable source, and what's more reliable than the people who are making the rules?

Department of Public Safety Texas Driver License Overview

This is where you're going to find all of the information that you need about your driver's license in Texas. It has everything about each type of license, how to get it, what you need, frequently asked questions, identification, and more. If you have a question about your license, this is the first place you should be going to get the answers.

Texas Department of Licensing & Regulation Driver Education and Safety

This is the second-best place you should be going when it comes to getting information about driving and driver education. You'll be able to find information about classes, instructors, verification, certificates, and even parent-led programs. All of the information you need will be located here, or you can be directed to other websites with the information you need.

Texas Department of Public Safety Choosing a Driver Education Course

When it comes to taking a driver education course, you want to make sure you're getting a quality one, and the Texas Department of Public Safety can help you choose exactly what you need. This page is where you'll find information about the different types of courses that are approved by the DPS.

Texas Department of Public Safety How to Prepare for a Drive Test checklist

This page will give you a checklist of just how you can prepare for your drive test. It goes over safety tips as well as a safety checklist and vehicle inspection. Not only that, but it shows you what you will be asked to do while you are completing the driving portion of your exam so you can prepare with a parent or other licensed driver beforehand.

With the help of any combination of these resources, you should be better prepared for your Texas driver's license exam and the driving portion of your test. You can check out any collection from these resources whether you're looking for free or paid options.

CONCLUSION

Preparing for the Texas Drivers Test requires you to be fully prepared. That means making sure that you know what to expect from both the written portion and the driving portion. It also means making sure that you take the time to figure out what are the best ways for you to learn and study. And then making sure that you follow through on them.

With this guide, you should feel confident about the process of preparing for and getting your Texas drivers license. All you have to do is read through and practice the study questions. You'll be ready in no time and you're going to be more than comfortable walking into the DPS to get your drivers license.

REFERENCES

www.houstontx.gov/courts/pdf/fineschedule_0110.pdf

https://www.google.com/url?sa=t&rct=j&q=&esrc=s&source=web&cd=&cad=rja&uact=8&ved=2ahUKEwizwcC5-fPsAhUOac0KHZv-A-UQFjABegQIBRAC&url=https%3A%2F%2Fwww.athensreview.com%2Fnews%2Ftexas-among-strictest-in-reckless-driving-cases%2Farticle_5e77bd66-8163-11e8-999f-df3f24ac551d.html&usg=AOvVaw2l511VDaA9YAEqnwvH1d8l

https://www.defensivedriving.com/blog/the-10-most-commonly-broken-driving-laws-in-texas-and-how-to-avoid-them/

https://teendriving.aaa.com/TX/supervised-driving/licensing-and-state-laws/

156 | REFERENCES

https://www.idrivesafely.com/dmv/texas/learners-permit/driving-test-guide/

https://driversed.com/texas/driving-lessons/driving-test-mistakes-to-avoid.aspx

https://www.dps.texas.gov/internetforms/forms/dl-60.pdf

https://driving-tests.org/texas/texas-permit-practice-test/

https://driving-tests.org/texas/dmv-written-test/

https://driving-tests.org/texas/texas-permit-practice-test-3/

https://driving-tests.org/texas/dmv-practice-test/

https://driving-tests.org/road-sign-test/

https://dmv-permit-test.com/texas/practice-test-1.html

https://dmv-permit-test.com/texas/practice-test-2.html

https://dmv-permit-test.com/texas/practice-test-3.html

https://dmv-permit-test.com/texas/practice-test-4.html

http://www.texasdrivereducation.us/practice-test/

https://www.dmv-written-test.com/texas/practice-test-1.html#

https://www.dmv-written-test.com/texas/practice-test-2.html#

https://www.dmv-written-test.com/texas/practice-test-3.html

https://www.dmv-written-test.com/texas/practice-test-4.html

https://www.dmv-written-test.com/texas/practice-test-5.html

https://www.dmv-written-test.com/texas/practice-test-6.html

https://www.dmv-written-test.com/texas/practice-test-7.html